From Vision to Fruition

Lessons from the book of

Nehemiah

Pastor Jack Abeelen

Published by Morningstar Christian Chapel
ISBN-13: 978-0-9964131-0-7
ISBN-10: 0-9964131-0-3

All scriptures are taken from the New King James Version of the Bible, unless otherwise indicated. Translational emendations, amplifications, and paraphrases are by the author.

Additional copies of this book are available by contacting:

Morningstar Christian Chapel
16241 Leffingwell Road, Whittier, California, 90603

The Chapel Store
562-943-0357

From Vision to Fruition

Lessons from the book of Nehemiah

By Pastor Jack Abeelen

Contents

Foreword

By Pastor Dave Rolph

The book of Nehemiah is the account of one of the most fascinating periods of Hebrew history, and features the leadership of one of the most interesting men in the Bible. Following the Assyrian and Babylonian captivities, the children of Israel faced overwhelming odds if they were to survive as a civilization and a religion. Their attempts to repopulate and rebuild their capital city of Jerusalem had fallen flat. What they needed was an inspirational leader who could capture the imagination of the people sufficiently to unite them in establishing a foundation for their future. The man God raised up for this task was an unlikely hero named Nehemiah. Nehemiah wasn't a prophet, priest, or king. He had no miraculous powers, but he had a heart for God and a determination to get things done, and that was plenty.

In this commentary, Pastor Jack Abeelen takes us on a verse by verse journey through the book of Nehemiah, relaying this fascinating story with special attention given to its application for leadership in the church today. There is an abundance of literature that has been published to address leadership within the church. Most of these books are approaching leadership from a secular viewpoint, applying business principles to the church based on what seems to work. This book doesn't take that approach. Jack analyzes the story of Nehemiah, and the leadership principles found therein, and weaves throughout the story many other Scriptures that support the leadership lessons of Nehemiah. Thus, it is not just isolated conclusions drawn from one book of the Bible, but a comprehensive treatment of biblical leadership from the entire Bible with a spotlight on Nehemiah. It is thoroughly practical for anyone involved in Christian leadership in any context.

Jack Abeelen is a highly effective communicator of the Scriptures, as can be attested by the many thousands of people who listen to his nationwide daily radio broadcasts on Growing Thru Grace and who attend his church, Morningstar Christian Chapel. There are many good Bible teachers out there, but Jack stands out for me because he is a man who isn't playing a part or conducting a performance. When Jack talks about the leadership principles of Nehemiah he is talking about, not only what he believes, but what he practices. I enjoyed reading this book not just because of what it says, as good as that is, but because of who is saying it. Jack is a man who practices what he preaches, which gives this book special value.

May God use this book to inspire you in your service to God as you seek to lead His people in whatever capacity to which He calls you.

–Pastor Dave Rolph
Senior Pastor, Calvary Chapel Pacific Hills
Teacher, The Balanced Word Radio Ministry

Acknowledgments

By Pastor Jack Abeelen

It is such a joy for me to sit in front of a computer and write out these studies and commentaries as God has so graciously taught me over these may years. Yet the vision for them did not start with me. Years ago, my good friend Nikki Smith came and shared her heart with me regarding the publishing of my Bible studies. Her great dedication over the years to transcribe, rewrite, edit, and dedicate herself to that vision is the reason these books have become a reality. Her love for Jesus, His Word, and for my ministry has continued to provide the tools necessary to publish these various studies.

Additionally I want to thank Pastor Brian Procedo for his layout and graphics work. His gift to be able to communicate in that way is a sure sign of God's hand upon him. Our secretary, Tara Boehm, worked long hours proof reading, making editing suggestions, and taking great interest in this finished work. Her fingerprints can be lovingly found on nearly every page. A thank you also to Pastor Ron Kitchell, our children's ministry pastor, who has a penchant for writing and provided many wonderful suggestions and helps in bringing this commentary to print. My wife, Debbie, should get the credit for what you find here, her love and support, encouragement and unwavering faith are a bedrock in our home and a blessing to me each day.

My good friend, Pastor Dave Rolph, was kind enough to provide the foreword for this study. His example, teaching, and years of friendship have had a profound effect on my walk with Jesus and my outlook as a pastor serving His flock. He is the real deal and I am blessed to know him and have access to his counsel.

Finally, to the body of believers that comprise the

church I have the privilege to pastor, Morningstar Christian Chapel, thank you for your great love and support, kindness and grace that you have extended to me, my family, and staff over the past 30+ years. It is a joy serving you and with you and the satisfaction of my heart has been to watch one generation and then another step up and begin serving the Lord we so love. You guys are the best!

–Pastor Jack Abeelen

Part One

Rebuilding

Chapter 1

Introduction To The Book Of Nehemiah

Nehemiah is certainly one of my favorite books of the Old Testament. Through it, I have learned how to better discover the will of God for my life. I have seen how ministry should be carried forth and what I can expect when I begin to step out in faith to serve the Lord. Nehemiah's journal is a handbook for pastors, church planters, and missionaries. It will provide lessons on preparation for the ministry, set before you the balance between planning and faith, and assure you of both opposition and victory. It will speak to you about how to wait upon the Lord and why sometimes we must prayerfully wait longer than we had hoped, seeking God impatiently while heaven remains silent. From God's providence, timing, oversight, and guidance to our preparation and work, Nehemiah's writings overflow with wisdom and example, and comfort and direction. It is a book I return to often, a book I teach to our graduating Bible school students, and one I cling to as I seek to know God, and serve Him and His people. I know it is going to radically contribute to your walk and work in His kingdom.

We first meet Nehemiah at work in a very powerful position in the Medo-Persian Empire as the king's food taster or cup-bearer. Eventually God will send him to rebuild Jerusalem's walls to provide protection and dignity for God's people, and restore them to a faithful walk with Him. Then we will see him promoted by the king as governor over Judea. It is that very journey, from cup-bearer to builder to ruler, which provides the backdrop for our learning. What is God's will for my life? What about the impossibilities I face? Can God use me? Why do I pray and He does not answer? How should I respond to criticism, the judgments of others, and even the cost involved in serving the Lord?

All of these are difficult questions and challenges that Nehemiah faced and, with him, we will get answers to each and every one of our concerns. Nehemiah will also teach us that God works mightily in, what we might label, very uneventful ways. We can all recognize His hand when something spectacular occurs. But in the book of Nehemiah, unless you're watching carefully, you can miss the fact that God has just done something great. We will need spiritual vision to see what God is doing and Nehemiah had his eyes constantly upon his God. In 2 Kings 6, Elisha and his servant, Gehazi, were surrounded by their enemy, the Syrians. "We're done," Gehazi said. "Look at all those soldiers, we don't stand a chance!" Elisha prayed that God would open the eyes of his servant so he might clearly see the Lord's army surrounding them. When Gehazi looked again and saw the angels of the Lord camped around them, he saw things from an entirely different perspective. Elisha had spiritual vision, while Gehazi was given it by the Lord. Nehemiah went through much that same process as God gave him spiritual vision and he would go share that with others.

Nehemiah is a wonderful book about helping others rise to their full potential in the Lord. If leadership is influence, then you are only as good of a leader as the fruit your leadership produces. Nehemiah is a God-ordained leader who received a vision from Him, was able to share that vision with many others, and then Nehemiah and his followers brought glory and honor to God and His people in Jerusalem.

I pray our study through this book together will do much to bring you to that place for which God is preparing you today. Nehemiah begins with a man of God brokenhearted, on his knees, and seeking His face. As we start our studies together, may we also cry out to our Lord to speak to us and make His ways known so we might serve Him mightily in these last days. The work before us is formidable, but Nehemiah will convince us that the availability of a single man who has surrendered to God can lead to the restoring faith of an entire nation.

Chapter 2

Background And Context

By way of context, Ezra chapters 1-6 give us much information regarding the repatriation of Israel from their captivity in Babylon in 536 BC. In that year, Cyrus, the Medo-Persian king, invited the nation of Israel to return to their homeland and about 50,000 Jews headed home. They arrived at a city that had been leveled and overrun, lying in rubble. Their first order of business was to rebuild the temple because that was the place of God's presence among His people and the place they could meet with Him through sacrifice and offerings. The foundation for the temple was soon laid, but complaints from surrounding enemies to the king began soon after and the work was interrupted for a time. That and the extremely tough living conditions caused the people to turn their focus to building their own houses first, setting aside the work on God's house for 16 years. At that time, God sent Haggai, Zechariah, and others to call them back to the work of His temple and fellowship with Him. Their message was plain and simple: "You have been here 16 years and have built for yourself fancy places to live while the house of God, the place of meeting, still lies in shambles." He told them through the prophet Haggai that their labors for gain had been frustrated and that their need for rain and blessings had been purposefully held back by the Lord, because they had been holding back from serving Him. He declared they were putting their money into pockets with holes in them, all their hopes had been unrealized, and what they had gained had not lasted. He also declared that they should seriously consider their ways, come back to the Lord, put Him first, and all of their needs would be met (Haggai 1:6-7)!

They got the message and took it to heart and were soon back to the building of the temple. Four years later, in 516 BC, the work was completed and worship began anew with fervor and joy. As promised, God faithfully met every need of these pioneers and His blessings followed. Some 60 years later, Ezra would bring a group of about 2,000 men from Babylon to minister in the temple, to help with worship, and to gather the folks together for sacrifice. He brought spiritual encouragement and organization to the place of worship. Twelve years later, in 446 BC, Nehemiah would arrive in Jerusalem, about 90 years after that first group of 50,000 had headed home. The city still had no walls of protection nor roads to accommodate travel. The walls had been down 140 years, since 586 BC, when Nebuchadnezzar had leveled the city. The nation was living in desolation and shame and Nehemiah would be God's man to lead the charge to make a difference. His calling, sending, and work is what the pages of this book are all about. From him, we will learn what God can do with the likes of us.

Chapter 3

God's Work Begins In The Heart

Nehemiah 1

The words of Nehemiah the son of Hachaliah. It came to pass in the month of Chislev, in the twentieth year, as I was in Shushan the citadel, that Hanani one of my brethren came with men from Judah; and I asked them concerning the Jews who had escaped, who had survived the captivity, and concerning Jerusalem. And they said to me, "The survivors who are left from the captivity in the province are there in great distress and reproach. The wall of Jerusalem is also broken down, and its gates are burned with fire."

–Nehemiah 1:1-3

Nehemiah's name translates as "Jehovah comforts" or "God is my comforter." His father's name was Hachaliah or "God has enlightened me." Only 50,000 people had taken the opportunity to return to Jerusalem in 536 BC. Most deemed Babylonian life superior to the rural frontier of Jerusalem. The people would rather live in this idolatrous place than in the city where God placed His name. About 90 years later, we are introduced to a family whose very names suggest they had a relationship with God and longed to serve Him. Nehemiah's family had been born in captivity. He himself had never seen Jerusalem. He had never been to the temple of God to worship. But in his heart burned a great love for the people of God and for His city, the place He had chosen to put His name. Jerusalem had no protection, and was a laughingstock and chattel to the powerful of the area. Yet hundreds of miles away in the life of a young man born into a godly family, the work of God's Spirit had begun to stir a heart.

We read in verse 1 that it was in the 20th year of the rule of, who we know to be, Artaxerxes Longimanus that our story begins. The month Chislev is the ninth month of the Jewish calendar, or November or December in ours. So in the winter of 446 BC, Nehemiah was living in Shushan at the citadel, the royal palace, which today would be found on the Persian Gulf of Iran, about 750 miles from Jerusalem.

As we will learn from verse 11, Nehemiah was the king's food taster. It was a job filled with danger and yet a trusted position, for Nehemiah tasted the king's food to see if it was poisoned before it was served to him. If it was, Nehemiah would be the one to take the bullet. Yet the king needed to trust Nehemiah was not involved in some conspiracy to have him killed. The word "brethren" in verse 2 can refer to an actual blood brother and it would appear from Nehemiah 7:2 that Hanani might very well have been Nehemiah's real brother who, for some reason, had been able to travel to Jerusalem. Upon Hanani's return, Nehemiah was full of questions for him. How are the people? How are they doing? How's the situation there for them? In Nehemiah's heart, God had stirred concern and he wanted to know about everything – about the survivors, the suffering, and the city. The news would not be good.

We meet Nehemiah working as a captive in a powerful position and learn immediately that his heart was breaking to see God begin a work where suffering, difficulty, and hopelessness abounded. I would suggest to you that this is always the way God's call to ministry for an individual begins. It begins in your heart! So often we find those who have a calling or concern for a particular ministry working hard at trying to make others care as they do. Emotional videos are produced, passionate pleas are made, and hopefully moved hearts are enlisted to "join" in the work. However, unless God moves the heart, that help will be temporary and require constant encouragement and cheerleading to continue. I personally am happy to simply seek God and allow Him to form my heart to desire what He wants for my life. What would happen if all of us were called to the same place? There would be hundreds of ushers, but no one to seat; hundreds standing in the pulpit, but no one to teach. I love our missionaries, pray for them often, and long for their fruitfulness, but I know I am not called to the mission field; I was called to a pastorate. If you really want to know what God is calling you to do, look at what breaks your heart.

When Paul wrote to Timothy, he said, "This is a faithful saying: If a man desires the position of a bishop, he desires a good work" (1 Timothy 3:1). The word "desire" speaks of a longing from within, a work of God in the heart of one who belongs to Him. Not everyone is longing to be placed in the position of an overseer, but those who do desire a good thing. Paul, writing to the Corinthians, said, "For if I preach the gospel, I have nothing to boast of, for necessity is laid upon me; yes, woe is me if I do not preach the gospel!" (1 Corinthians 9:16). His point is that he hadn't chosen that ministry for himself but rather God had placed it in his heart.

The implication of knowing this truth is revolutionary, for if you believe that God begins the work of the ministry in the heart, you can never really go about seeking to force concern in others for the work God is beginning to do in your heart. If their concern is missing, probably their calling to that is as well. Nehemiah's heart was being churned by the Lord and nothing would deter him from seeking to do what God had placed in him. We can share our concerns, share the vision God has given us, and hope others will join us, but it must begin as a work of God in the heart of an individual.

We have had people call the church to share their burdens with us. It often begins with a phone call, "Could I talk to the pastor?" When I answer the phone, this is what I hear:

"Do you know what we need?" They will then begin to lay out for me something that God is really stirring their hearts about and they'll say, "Don't you think we need that?" "No," I'll respond, "but if you do, why don't you start praying about how you can implement that in the life of the body here?" "Oh, no, pastor," they reply. "You don't understand. I don't have the time for this. That's your job, not mine! I just wanted to give you some direction!" Learn that God's work must begin in an individual's heart, just as Nehemiah was churning for Jerusalem and the well-being of its citizens.

In verse 3, Hanani gives Nehemiah the bad news. The survivors who had returned here 90 years earlier are living a destitute existence. The walls that used to protect the city, torn down by Nebuchadnezzar 140 years earlier, had never been restored. As a result, the people of God were living in "distress and reproach." The rogues and thieves around the city were making life for these pilgrims miserable and there were no plans to improve conditions for them.

> *So it was, when I heard these words, that I sat down and wept, and mourned for many days; I was fasting and praying before the God of heaven.*
>
> *–Nehemiah 1:4*

If the first step of discovering what God wants you to do is to determine what He's speaking to your heart, then the second step is determining what breaks your heart, making that calling clear. Here, Nehemiah was in tears by himself. There was no one that sought to prey on his emotions. There were no sales pitches or any peer pressure. It was Nehemiah by himself – a young man touched by God – whose heart was breaking. He knew something had to be done.

But first Nehemiah weeps as would Daniel, Habakkuk, Jeremiah, and others. He'd heard enough and now needed to begin to seek God as to how to fix it. But it was this drastic work in his heart that brought this man of God to tears and to his knees.

When you want to find out what God might want to do through you, ask yourself what you care about most. The best person to lighten any load is the one who has felt the pressure of it himself. I think the tragedy you find in churches sometimes is that people believe that God is somehow most interested in the biggest, whether it be the biggest vision, the biggest need, or the biggest number. People become attracted to that. But the moment you set out to do great things for God is the moment you've lost your way when it comes to His calling. If Nehemiah was going to build the wall, he was first going to have to weep over the ruins. That is always the case when it comes to ministry.

I have found that the folks who are truly touched by a need are the first to show up to help and the last to leave. They'll bend over backwards, give you the shirt off their back, and not be able to get enough of the ministry God has set before them. Find folks with that compassion and you'll find ministry that will last. They will not need constant reassuring they are doing God's work. They know it because God has brought them and they would have come even if they had to come alone. When I watch saints serve in places of true calling, their passion thrills my heart and I see God's hand at work in them and through them. You must ask yourself what's burning in your heart. Unless you're serving where God is burning within, you will eventually lose interest and move on. We need a work of God in our hearts, a concern that leads to mourning, and mourning that leads to moving – but the despair has to come before the determination. Find out what God is doing in your heart, whether it's going to the mission field, visiting the prisoners, spending time with the poor, or preaching in the streets – it doesn't matter. There's not one better than the other. It's just a matter of what God wants for you.

So we read here of Nehemiah weeping and mourning, fasting and praying. The news absolutely broke his heart. Fasting usually requires stress. It is most often found in the Scriptures being practiced by people repenting of their sins. But it is also found in those who need, from the bottom of their hearts, to hear from God. It is the intensity Nehemiah felt that drove him to fast. Nehemiah wasn't the first guy in the Bible to weep over Jerusalem, and he wouldn't be the last. Jeremiah would sit upon the hill outside of town for months and weep. On the Mount of Olives, the week before He was to die for our sins, Jesus wept for the people – wept over their unwillingness to hear from Him and wept over the impending consequences of their choices. Here, this high-ranking official with a tender heart hears about the condition of the city and it left him in tears and in great distress before his Lord. In that position, he turns to God to see what God might want to do with him. We start by looking to see what God is saying to us, which is clarified by what is breaking our hearts, and from there we turn back to Him to find His help and direction to accomplish His will.

> *And I said: "I pray, LORD God of heaven, O great and awesome God, You who keep Your covenant and mercy with those who love You and observe Your commandments, please let Your ear be attentive and Your eyes open, that You may hear the prayer of Your servant which I pray before You now, day and night, for the children of Israel Your servants, and confess the sins of the children of Israel which we have sinned against You. Both my father's house and I have sinned. We have acted very corruptly against You, and have not kept the commandments, the statutes, nor the ordinances which You commanded Your servant Moses."*
>
> *–Nehemiah 1:5-7*

Put yourself in Nehemiah's shoes. He's working for a king who is an absolute monarch, which means that if he wants you dead, he kills you – and then has lunch. He answers to no one. Nehemiah is 750 miles away from Jerusalem, the place of his concern, a place he'd never been. He's going to need lots of time away from his present job, a king who is on board with the work, huge amounts of materials, and a labor force that will work to build a wall while surrounded by enemies. Those enemies will not take too kindly to anyone protecting these families they have been able to take advantage of for years. Then there is the lethargy of the people themselves – four generations who had lived and died there without any movement to improve their lot.

Nehemiah might as well have wanted to go to Mars. The situation in Jerusalem that was breaking his heart was intolerable, but what could he do? God is stirring his heart for Jerusalem and its inhabitants, but now he felt helpless. Nehemiah is wise though; he turns to the Lord for help. The next step in finding God's will for your life is to seek Him regarding how to move forward when His direction becomes clear. Nehemiah seeks the Lord to find out how He's going to open the doors for him. Rather than despair over the seemingly insurmountable task before him, Nehemiah turned to the Lord. If God is stirring and breaking your heart, He's big enough to guide you and help you finish the work. Your confidence in Him is absolutely vital if you're going to remain in a position where He can use you. So Nehemiah begins to pray and that would be his posture, as we will learn, for the next four months.

Notice Nehemiah begins by asking God for help and immediately confesses the sin of his people and of himself. It was in 606 BC, due to their ongoing unrepentant idolatry, when the Lord allowed the southern kingdom of Judah to be overthrown by the Babylonians and carried 750 miles away to live under a regime that worshiped hundreds of different gods. Although neither Nehemiah nor his father were alive back then, Nehemiah joined in responsibility for the nation's sin. I love the fact that, rather than blaming others, Nehemiah just said, "It's me." In using the pronoun "we," Nehemiah confesses his own sinfulness and need. He didn't come to the

Lord, saying, "Lord, You owe me this," because God owed him nothing. No, he said, "I know who You are and You know who I am. I need Your help. I know the difficulty is ours, but the solution has to be Yours." Nehemiah confesses his sin. He couldn't change the nation, but he could be responsible for himself and he confessed his need. He desired to receive God's blessing but he came with empty hands. He didn't come demanding. He came humbly.

He then appeals in prayer to God's faithfulness rather than to his own.

> *"Remember, I pray, the word that You commanded Your servant Moses, saying, 'If you are unfaithful, I will scatter you among the nations; but if you return to Me, and keep My commandments and do them, though some of you were cast out to the farthest part of the heavens, yet I will gather them from there, and bring them to the place which I have chosen as a dwelling for My name.' Now these are Your servants and Your people, whom You have redeemed by Your great power, and by Your strong hand."*
>
> *–Nehemiah 1:8-10*

Not only did Nehemiah go to the Word of God to find out the cause of Judah's problems, but he also continued in the Word to find the solution. I think a good rule of thumb when you're learning to pray – especially if you're praying specifically about what God might want from your life – is to pray with a Bible next to you. Point to verses of God's promises and say, "Look, Lord, what You said." Now, God doesn't need to be reminded of His promises, but you do. And though you are in a position to demand nothing, you are in a very favorable position to hang on to His wonderful word of promise, which God will make sure for you. Nehemiah came with empty hands, but he did not come uninvited! God loves it when we seek Him in prayer.

It's important that when God begins to stir your heart, that your position has to be one of humility before God, looking for His work, and reminding yourself of what God has promised. You can't do anything about other people. Nobody seems to care. That's all right. Do you care? No one seems to be involved. Sorry. How about you?

> *"O Lord, I pray, please let Your ear be attentive to the prayer of Your servant, and to the prayer of Your servants who desire to fear Your name; and let Your servant prosper this day, I pray, and grant him mercy in the sight of this man." For I was the king's cupbearer.*
> *–Nehemiah 1:11*

Finally, the fourth step in discovering what God would have you do is found here in verse 11: Be available to fill the need you see. There are plenty of voices to be found in any church that will gripe about what the church does not have and what it needs, what should or should not have been done. Nehemiah was not one of those people. He just desired to be a part of the solution and his prayer put things into clear perspective. He calls the king, the most powerful man on the planet, "this man" in verse 11. In other words, Nehemiah didn't lose sight of who was actually sitting on the throne.

It is important when you make yourself available, you don't fall prey to the lies of the enemy, who will seek to tell you that you don't have what it takes. "You don't have enough education," he'll say. "You don't have enough money. You don't have enough time. You don't have enough help. Who do you think you are?" Tasting food for a living didn't really qualify Nehemiah for wall building, construction, organization, community organizing, motivating, or any form of political oversight. But he was available and that's all God requires. If you can submit to the Lord, God can use you to accomplish His will. Since I read that God even spoke through donkeys, I conclude we can all be useful to Him if we will simply make ourselves available to be part of the answer to our prayers.

Would God answer Nehemiah's prayer? Yes, but not immediately. In fact, between chapters 1 and 2, some four months will pass with absolutely no word from heaven. One of the big lessons from the book of Nehemiah is God's timing is always perfect. Why did He make Nehemiah wait and why does He make us wait? We will learn that waiting will sharpen our focus and deepen our calling and commitment. If the Lord allowed us to immediately do whatever we were emotionally involved with, we'd often go off in the wrong direction. It takes time to see clearly and waiting accomplishes that. Waiting develops our faith and allows us to plan. And in chapter 2, we'll see that planning is exactly what Nehemiah did; planning by faith for four long months. What would I do or need if God should open those doors?

So the calling of God begins in an individual life and can often be clearly determined by what breaks your heart. In that brokenness we then turn to seek God's hand in prayer for open doors, wisdom to continue, and confession of our need. Finally, as we are willing to be the vessel through whom He might work, we find ourselves on the path to both finding and walking in His plans for our lives.

Chapter 4

A Vision In The Making, Working While Waiting

Nehemiah 2

And it came to pass in the month of Nisan, in the twentieth year of King Artaxerxes, when wine was before him, that I took the wine and gave it to the king. Now I had never been sad in his presence before.

–Nehemiah 2:1

I think all of us have had to deal with authorities in our lives whose influence seemed to have control over us, whether we liked it or not. As a child, your parents were in charge of you and your ways. In school, your teachers were an authority figure in your life. Then you go to work and your employers tell you what to do. Then you get married and – well, you get the picture. Here Nehemiah works for an unbeliever, a king who lives to serve himself, driven by selfish gain. Yet he would have to go through him to get to where God wanted him to be, 750 miles to Jerusalem, building a wall with government funds.

Hudson Taylor, founder of the Inland China Mission, wrote of the trials he faced in dealing with the Chinese government – the changes of opinion and the difficulty of simply getting a straight answer. He said, "I have learned it is possible to move men simply through prayer." Without any kind of worldly tactics of intimidation, without anger or threats, God's will can be accomplished even in the most wicked, resistant lives simply through the prayers of His people. That's where

Nehemiah finds himself. If he was ever going to be allowed to pursue what God had placed on his heart, God's hand was going to have to touch the heart of the man who stood in his way. He was a big man and it seemed like a hard way.

I guess in one sense this was easy for Nehemiah since there was really nothing else he could do. Unfortunately for us, there are all kinds of other things we can do, so we usually try them all before looking to God for help. At least Nehemiah started with God. There was no other place or person to whom he could turn. He loved the people. He loved the city. God had broken his heart and it filled his prayer time. He'd even gone without food for the sake of praying for them. And pray he did. Verse 2:1 tells us he had been praying for quite a while. In fact, back in verse 1:1, we learned that it was in the month of Chislev that God began to stir his heart – November or December. Now it's the month Nisan, April. Nearly five months have passed and so far nothing had changed.

If you are of the opinion that God in the Bible answered the prayers of His people immediately and that the only thing we lack is that we don't live in biblical days, you haven't read the entire Bible. Nehemiah is but one example of many who came to God with specific prayers having been moved by a work of God in their hearts. He came to God with much prayer, often accompanied with the denying of the flesh in fasting, with great humility, and many tears; and still God did not quickly answer him. For a full third of a year, there had been absolutely no indication God was even listening. It's as if heaven was closed.

Although four months have passed since God first stirred Nehemiah's heart and he began to pray, nothing had changed. We find Nehemiah still hurting. His prayers are still being offered with weeping and sorrow. The people in Jerusalem were still living in miserable conditions. God still isn't responding. Learn from Nehemiah that if God has stirred your heart, you should not quit praying or give up because God seems slow to action. I asked a brother in our body how things were going in his life and he told me of several months of unanswered prayer and concluded by saying, "I'm going to give God one more week to direct me." I thought to myself, "Oh, yeah, that's going to put the fear of God in God!"

How well do we wait when God is not quick to answer? Isaiah 65:24 is one of my favorite verses. It says, "It shall come to pass That before they call, I will answer; And while they are speaking, I will hear." I love that verse. Unfortunately, it doesn't occur very often in Scripture or in life. More often than not, there is a waiting period between the time God stirs a heart and the time He opens the doors for a work to begin.

It's easy to wait upon God when you don't care about something. But if your heart is like Nehemiah's, the waiting can be excruciating. Some people will try to earn a response from God, hoping He works like the world around us. "God, if I go to church an extra day, will that help? How about five extra dollars in the offering plate?" Or we try to make a deal with God. "If You do this for me, here's what I'll do for You …" Sometimes we just fall for the lies of the devil who tells us, "God listens to everyone's prayers but yours. So get lost." Why does God have us wait? If you look into the Bible you will find many reasons in the lives of those who prayed and waited as to why they had to wait. Sometimes the waiting is simply to weed out the "not called." All of us, because we are saved, are tender in heart toward suffering. It isn't necessarily a quality of the lost, but it is absolutely a criterion of the saint. So if you see a little child on TV that's not eating, you immediately are drawn to try to help. That's just what God does in your heart. If someone's out of their home, you want to build one for them. If someone is being taken advantage of, you want to come to their defense. All of those emotional responses to need are certainly the Lord's tenderness in your heart, but they don't constitute a specific call.

If we can wait between the calling of God and the open doors of fulfillment, we will discover there comes from waiting a tremendous inner assurance of calling. Often people respond to a felt need by wanting to get involved with the last missionary they heard speak. "I'm moving to Zimbabwe." But then the next speaker comes along and he lives in upstate NY. "That's what I meant to say." In their emotional response they are pulled in many different directions. Waiting upon God winnows the field.

Additionally, delays in answers to prayer will force you to continue to pray. If God always answered immediately, you wouldn't develop much confidence in prayer. You'd simply ask and get and ask again for more. But what happens when God makes you wait? You have to either become convinced God hears and His timing is perfect, or you eventually give up. Dependency upon God can only be developed when you find that you're dependent upon Him, not upon His answer. Let me illustrate that for you.

Hannah, the wife of Elkanah who had been barren, prayed for years to have a child. Each year at the temple she came with reasons why God should allow her to have children. One day she stood before Him and her attitude and reasons had changed. She now just wanted to honor the Lord and have her child, a son, serve Him all of his life. She prayed "Lord, if You give me a child, I will give that child back to You to serve You all the days of his life." That's exactly what God wanted to hear and when He did, she became pregnant and gave birth to Samuel (1 Samuel 1).

In Luke 18:1, Luke wrote that Jesus began to speak a parable to His men with the purpose of teaching them that men always ought to pray and never to lose heart. He then told the parable of the unjust judge. It was a picture of a judge who was old and cranky but in power. He didn't fear God nor consider man. He really couldn't care less about anyone. But a widow who didn't feel like she'd been treated properly came to him for help. True to form, he quickly dispensed of her. So she took a new tack. She came every day. Knock. Knock. Knock. "It's me again. Remember me? How are things? Can you help me today?" Every day she came. This unjust judge became so bothered by this pestering that Jesus said it was only to shut this woman up that he decided to help her. He didn't help her because he cared for her; he helped her because he cared only for himself. Then Jesus said, "Hear what the unjust judge said. And shall God not avenge His own elect who cry out day and night to Him, though He bears long with them? I tell you that He will avenge them speedily. Nevertheless, when the Son of Man comes, will He really find faith on the earth?" (Luke 18:6-8). In other words, if you can badger an unbelieving, wicked person into helping you for his own sake, how much more is God on your side when you pray, looking for His help and care? God's heart is always ready to answer you. Therefore, if there's a delay, it's because He's working things out for our benefit.

But there is at least one other reason for waiting and we find it specifically here in Nehemiah 2. While we wait, God would have us plan. One purpose in all of this waiting upon God is that you and I might take that time to begin to develop what we would do or need if and when He opens the door. Nehemiah is a perfect example of waiting, praying, and planning, being "pray-pared." He counts the cost. He thinks through the process. He focuses on the needs he would have, how long it would take him, and what he would need in terms of support so when God opened the door, Nehemiah could say, "Here's what the Lord has been showing me." He was working while he was waiting, not just sitting around complaining that he had to wait so long.

I am sure that God will not stir your heart to the point He did Nehemiah's without also providing you an opportunity to accomplish the work. However, His timing is His, not yours. You may have to wait for Him to open the door, but there will be plenty to do while you wait. Nehemiah would spend four months fasting and praying, faithfully going to work every day, and leaving his concerns with God. Verse 1 tells us Nehemiah had not one time shown up for work carrying the burdens of his heart upon his face. Yet one day, serving the king his wine after dinner, Nehemiah did not appear his usual happy self and the perceptive king took notice and inquired of him why he had such a sad face that day.

> *Therefore the king said to me, "Why is your face sad, since you are not sick? This is nothing but sorrow of heart." So I became dreadfully afraid, and said to the king, "May the king live forever! Why should my face not be sad, when the city, the place of my fathers' tombs, lies waste, and its gates are burned with fire?"*
>
> *–Nehemiah 2:2-3*

To be sad in the presence of the king could be like signing your own death warrant (Proverbs 16:14). I'm sure at this point Nehemiah's life passed before his eyes. Nehemiah had not purposefully sought to reveal the broken heart he carried for Jerusalem and its people, but it was too late for that now. Maybe God was opening a door for him, or maybe the Lord was preparing to receive him into glory. Either way, he must tell him the truth! The danger was that past administrations had not spoken favorably of Jerusalem and certainly did not view it as a place that needed to be rebuilt. Nehemiah was not a rebellious person, but his heart was for his people and their city that lied in ruins. So Nehemiah told him the truth about the turmoil within his heart for the plight of Jerusalem, his ancestral home.

> *Then the king said to me, "What do you request?" So I prayed to the God of heaven. And I said to the king...*
>
> *–Nehemiah 2:4-5a*

Note the words in verse 2, "I became dreadfully afraid." Nehemiah was well aware of how the king might react, and yet this was the issue he had hoped to address with him one day. This was what he had been praying and fasting about all of these months. So without moving his lips, he tossed a quick prayer up before the Lord in his mind, in his heart, and then turned to speak to the king. There are many helpful books available on the subject of prayer. There are discussions about how often we should pray and about unanswered prayer. All of these are good topics to learn, but somehow I love how this short verse reduces prayer to its intended use: prayer is fellowship with God and a dependence upon Him. Nehemiah only has time to send a thought, a cry of help from within, to the Lord he depended upon.

The king asked Nehemiah what he wanted. Fortunately, Nehemiah had not spent the past four months of waiting doing nothing. He had been planning and now when asked, he had an answer for the king that contained concrete steps and requests. But the situation itself was frightening and Nehemiah looked to the Lord to go before him. After months of diligent fasting, tears, heartbreak, and prayer, the calling within to Jerusalem was as acute as ever. Nehemiah realized how important this conversation would be. So with a cry to the Lord he turned to speak to the king.

> *"If it pleases the king, and if your servant has found favor in your sight, I ask that you send me to Judah, to the city of my fathers' tombs, that I may rebuild it."*
> *–Nehemiah 2:5b*

"King, I want you to send me to my homeland. I want to put the walls back up in the city of my forefathers, I want to rebuild Jerusalem." Notice Nehemiah doesn't try to help God out. If this was me answering the king's question, I might have couched my request with 500 reasons why this would be good for the king and his kingdom as well. "Before I tell you what I want, let me tell you what this is going to do for you, O king. Let me tell you how happy you're going to be with the revenue, the accolades, and the tourism." I would become a salesman for my ideas and wishes.

But that's not what Nehemiah does. He just tells the king what he wants. If you can wait upon God like that, you're going to find God's best. And when you get to where God is bringing you, you'll never wonder whether you got there on your own or whether the Lord brought you there, because He will have opened every door. There are those who, by fund-raising and good salesmanship, find themselves successful, or so it seems, but it may be that when they say, "Look what the Lord has done!" that the Lord would say "I didn't do that!"

Nehemiah wasn't going to fall for self-promotion or worldly sales techniques. He doesn't couch his requests with lots of arguments or logic. He simply asks the king's permission to do what he believes God has called him to do, "if it pleases the king." He has faith that rests solely in God's work. Lord, give us that kind of trust in You!

Perhaps to Nehemiah's surprise, the king doesn't fall into a rage, but instead begins to ask several questions having to do with how long Nehemiah would be gone, and how long he would have to carry on without him by his side.

> *Then the king said to me (the queen also sitting beside him), "How long will your journey be? And when will you return?" So it pleased the king to send me; and I set him a time.*
>
> *–Nehemiah 2:6*

When the king asked Nehemiah, "How long will you be gone, when will you return," we realize it is really the same question asked two different ways. The king was startled a bit, I suspect, and the fact that we are told his wife, the queen, was sitting beside him might suggest she was partial to Nehemiah and was in fact encouraging his kindness to him. The important point is that Nehemiah was able to give him a defined answer, a time frame. We will learn later in the book (5:14) that Nehemiah would actually be gone for some 12 years. Whether or not he was able to anticipate such a long absence or not is hard to say, but for now he gives the king his best estimate of how long it might take. I want to drive this point home to you, for often people under a false sense of spirituality make no plans whatsoever and then call it faith.

I spoke a couple of years ago at a conference out of the country with a man who's fairly well known. "What are you speaking on this afternoon?" I asked him. "I don't know yet," he said. "The Lord will give me something." I must tell you I lost a great deal of respect for him that day, because I thought that if you're going to be brought across the ocean to speak to people who have paid to get you there, you ought to prepare yourself. I suspect God could have told him the week before what He wanted him to speak about. He didn't have to wait until the last minute. That isn't spiritual, that's irresponsible.

Walking by faith doesn't mean an absence of organization, it doesn't suggest a lack of planning and just moving along "as the Spirit leads," in fact, it is just the opposite. Nehemiah had spent four months crying out without answers – yet he was still making plans each day, being led by the Lord, illuminated by the Holy Spirit, with his heart still burning for the work.

So when the king said, "How long will you be gone?" Nehemiah was able to answer, "Here's how long I think I'll be gone." And the king will reply (8b), "That'll be fine. I can live with that." I think if Nehemiah had responded to the king by saying, "I don't know, whatever the Lord wants, He will show me when I get there," I suspect the king would have been far less willing to allow him to go at all. Zechariah wrote in 4:10 that we should not despise the day of small things. Indeed the Bible teaches us that if we are faithful in the little, God can give you much. Nehemiah had been doing the very thing I hope we can learn to do, and that is to prepare.

Proverbs 16:9 tells us: "A man's heart plans his way, But the LORD directs his steps." The presumption, of course, is that there is planning taking place on your end as you seek Him. God is stirring your heart and you're acting upon it.

You're not just sitting back saying, "I hope God does something." For example, if you desire God to lead you to a job, here's my advice: Go knock on doors. Go prayerfully. Go every day. I talked to a man out of work recently and asked him what he was dong about it. He said, "I called a guy this week." I said, "One call? You need to make finding a job your job. So get up every morning and go to work finding work. Pray as you go that God would lead you and look to Him for every meeting and possible open door. Your job is to find a job. Your job description: find a job. The Lord will go before you. But you must go knocking." Nehemiah was ready with an answer so that if ever God would see fit to open a door, Nehemiah would be ready to walk through it. The one thing Nehemiah could not afford was the luxury of not planning beforehand.

I have learned that planning is the hardest thing to teach people and it's the hardest thing to have them do. In Luke 14:28-32, Jesus said to His disciples, "For which of you, intending to build a tower, does not sit down first and count the cost, whether he has enough to finish it – lest, after he has laid the foundation, and is not able to finish, all who see it begin to mock him, saying, 'This man began to build and was not able to finish.' Or what king, going to make war against another king, does not sit down first and consider whether he is able with ten thousand to meet him who comes against him with twenty thousand? Or else, while the other is still a great way off, he sends a delegation and asks conditions of peace." The point is it is very spiritual and very biblical to plan ahead.

I teach several different studies each week. To do so well, I have to plan ahead. I don't know how else to do it! I believe in the moving of God's Spirit, and there are times when I use examples I never wrote down and use verses I didn't even know I knew – but I'm not going to rely just upon that. I'm going to be on my knees and praying and studying well to get answers the week before I am asked to come and speak for the Lord.

You can tell Nehemiah had planned every detail as he

not only has an idea of time commitment, he also has a shopping list of supplies needed to accomplish the work. He continues by asking the king for significant help from his surplus.

> *Furthermore I said to the king, "If it pleases the king, let letters be given to me for the governors of the region beyond the River, that they must permit me to pass through till I come to Judah, and a letter to Asaph the keeper of the king's forest, that he must give me timber to make beams for the gates of the citadel which pertains to the temple, for the city wall, and for the house that I will occupy." And the king granted them to me according to the good hand of my God upon me.*
>
> *–Nehemiah 2:7-8*

I love this! Nehemiah's request is bold but very practical. "I need safe passage to travel through Moab, Ammon, and other countries. I will need a signed visa that allows me free travel by your authority. Additionally, I am going to need your American Express card to use at your Home Depot because I am going to need lots of building supplies."

No doubt poor planning is a great frustration to any business, home, or church. Nehemiah was ready to answer. He didn't just react, but he anticipated what his needs might be. Nehemiah was ready with answers.

The Lord blessed and Nehemiah is well aware of the fact this open door and this willing king were the direct result of the goodness of God in going before him to prepare the way.

> *Then I went to the governors in the region beyond the River, and gave them the king's letters. Now the king had sent captains of the army and horsemen with me.*
>
> *–Nehemiah 2:9*

Nehemiah was given everything on his checklist. It was the king who then made a suggestion, contributing to the work, saying "Let me give you an army." I love the way God works. Manipulate and you'll probably get just as much as you can work. But wait upon God and you'll get much more than you thought possible – or, as Paul puts it in Ephesians 3:20, "exceedingly abundantly above all we ask or think."

Now Nehemiah has the finest army in the land protecting him and a royal entourage to give him safe passage. He couldn't have dreamed it or imagined it going any better. Soon he is off to Jerusalem to fulfill the calling of God upon his heart with the blessings of a heathen king whose heart God had touched.

> *When Sanballat the Horonite and Tobiah the Ammonite official heard of it, they were deeply disturbed that a man had come to seek the well-being of the children of Israel.*
>
> *–Nehemiah 2:10*

This glorious first section of chapter 2 ends on an ominous note and sets the stage for a recurring lesson we will discover in our study through Nehemiah: Whenever we begin to serve the Lord, we can expect opposition. Life is easier if you simply stay on the sidelines, but get into the game and you can expect the enemy to be gunning for you.

Sanballat and Tobiah had never met Nehemiah. They had only recently heard that a person who used to work for the king was now coming with a lot of clout to build a wall and bring protection to God's people in Jerusalem. Immediately they are deeply disturbed and angry that anyone was coming to their defense. They had no rhyme or reason, no knowledge of Nehemiah, just a general hatred for the things of God; it was spiritual warfare. We will learn from Nehemiah that we can handle opposition best when we are confident we are in the place God wants us to be and are doing what He desires from our life. The truth is that no one can stand in the way of God's good hand. We will see how the enemy comes against God's work and how Nehemiah finds God's strength and direction to continue to press ahead for His glory.

> *So I came to Jerusalem and was there three days. Then I arose in the night, I and a few men with me; I told no one what my God had put in my heart to do at Jerusalem; nor was there any animal with me, except the one on which I rode.*
>
> *–Nehemiah 2:11-12*

There is roughly a 3-month time gap found between verses 10 and 11, which represents the time required for planning and travel. When Nehemiah finally reaches Jerusalem, the first thing he needs to do is get a vision from the Lord of what the work is going to entail. He had been praying for months and had a list of what he thought he'd need, but he'd never seen the place. So this was his first chance to see how bad the damage really was. If I were Nehemiah, I'd want to start working right away. It's been the better part of a year that this had been burning in his heart. He had never seen Jerusalem though he had often read about the city in the Scriptures. He'd heard the description of the damage from friends and family who had come and gone, but now he would see it with his own eyes. So the first question in his heart: "Now that the Lord has brought me here, how do we go about doing this work?"

He was there for three days just waiting to see what the Lord might want to do. He wasn't frantic. He needed some rest to gather his thoughts and to assess the situation. He needed to have the Lord speak to him again to direct his next steps. If this was going to be a work of God, he was going to need the plan of God to accomplish it. He records that he went out on some secret scouting missions at night. He wanted to see the wall from every angle. He wanted to make sure he had a detailed understanding of the scope of the work before him.

He will mention a couple of times that he hadn't told

anyone yet what he had come to Jerusalem to do. I think it is a vital lesson to learn when seeking to lead others in ministry; you need to know what you're doing, where you are going, and how you plan to get there before seeking to get others involved. Nehemiah would first have to get the vision of how the work should now go forward. God had miraculously brought him this far, so Lord, what's next? So at night, Nehemiah travels alone, he travels light. He tells no one. It is this seeking of God quietly in the night for vision and direction that is the secret of good leadership and success in ministry. Get a vision from God!

I love the picture it paints for us. Nehemiah took some days of quiet, of little actual activity, prayerfulness, thoughtfulness, seeking clarity of thought, and direction of the Spirit. I personally think the greatest work is done right here where God is able to speak and place His ideas into the heart of this man He had called and chosen for the work. Not just emotion – because there had to have been great emotion involved in seeing the destruction, while caring so much for God's people – but planning, making good decisions, seeing the big picture, and hearing from God. If you don't do this first, you will never be able to anticipate potential problems and you will have little to share with people who ask you what you're doing. It's vital that this vision is first born in your heart.

By the way, this is not something you find only with Nehemiah. Prepared hearts who have been given a vision by the Lord are those who make good leaders and are found throughout the Scriptures. When Paul wrote to Timothy, his last letter to a man in his first pulpit, he said in 2 Timothy 2:15, "Be diligent to present yourself approved to God, a worker who does not need to be ashamed, rightly dividing the word of truth." In other words, "Prepare yourself, Timothy. Make sure you're ready to stand before the people."

David in conviction and repentance over his sin with Bathsheba prayed in Psalm 51:12-13, "Restore to me the joy of Your salvation, And uphold me by Your generous Spirit.

Then I will teach transgressors Your ways, And sinners shall be converted to You." David recognized it was only when he himself was walking with God that he could influence others to do the same.

In Ezra 7:10 we read that, "Ezra had prepared his heart to seek the Law of the LORD, and to do it, and to teach statutes and ordinances in Israel." Ezra received from God and walked in that which God had taught him before he began to teach others. That's always the way it is.

Paul, in writing his first letter to the Corinthians, spoke to them about the seriousness with which they should communion, an attitude which the church was slow to adopt. In 1 Corinthians 11:23, Paul begins by telling them, "For I received from the Lord that which I also delivered to you..." What I've received from the Lord is what I am now delivering to you. You cannot pass along to others what you have not received yourself. That's absolutely vital.

Early on in the book of Acts, the disciples were arrested for healing the lame man at the gate and for preaching the gospel of Jesus Christ. They were threatened and beaten by the Pharisees who told them they could no longer speak or preach in that name. The response of the disciples in Acts 4:20 tells us their lives had been touched by Him: "For we cannot but speak the things which we have seen and heard." The testimony of Jesus was now part of their lives. They couldn't deny the Lord. I love Nehemiah's example here because it had taken many miracles to bring him to this point. He could have simply assumed, but he could now decide what came next. He had been absolutely blessed to get here over the past months, but as yet no one knew about him or about God's plans. Nehemiah doesn't want to change managers now. So he rises up while everyone else is sleeping, seeking to know the heart of God, formulating a plan, and receiving a vision.

Leaders who want to make a difference need to get a vision from God before they go forward to call upon others to follow and labor with them in His work.

> *And I went out by night through the Valley Gate to the Serpent Well and the Refuse Gate, and viewed the walls of Jerusalem which were broken down and its gates which were burned with fire. Then I went on to the Fountain Gate and to the King's Pool, but there was no room for the animal under me to pass. So I went up in the night by the valley, and viewed the wall; then I turned back and entered by the Valley Gate, and so returned. And the officials did not know where I had gone or what I had done; I had not yet told the Jews, the priests, the nobles, the officials, or the others who did the work.*
>
> *–Nehemiah 2:13-16*

The word "viewed" (13,15) is a Hebrew word meaning to carefully inspect. I don't know how discouraged Nehemiah must have become seeing what up to now he had only imagined. There were places so filled with debris that he couldn't even ride his horse around them. Yet I don't find him saying, "Oh, man, this is worse than I thought." He is simply looking to familiarize himself with the details. He is making a list, covering the bases, traveling the perimeter of the city. If the reports back at the palace had brought him to tears, imagine what seeing them with his own eyes must have done to his heart.

Alan Redpath wrote a wonderful commentary on Nehemiah entitled Victorious Christian Living. Of this passage, he wrote, "When a real work of God is to be done, some faithful and burdened servant will have to take a long journey and weep in the night over the ruins." It is what stirs your heart, along with that compelling concern within that few others can share, that indeed defines the work of God. Just like in chapter 1, Nehemiah finds himself on his own again, still burdened by what he was concerned with months earlier. The nice thing was, now he was brokenhearted in Jerusalem, not somewhere

700 miles away. Having spent his time without telling anyone, discovering the vision from the Lord, and formulating a plan, it finally came time to involve others.

> *Then I said to them, "You see the distress that we are in, how Jerusalem lies waste, and its gates are burned with fire. Come and let us build the wall of Jerusalem, that we may no longer be a reproach."*
>
> *–Nehemiah 2:17*

Getting the vision eventually has to lead to sharing the vision God has given you if you are to ever see the work go forward. There are very few works of the Lord that are done alone. This certainly wasn't one of them. After four months of praying and fasting, three more of travel, and several days of viewing the rubble seeking the Lord; Nehemiah is now ready to share the vision with the Jews living in Jerusalem so that they might join him in the work God had placed upon his heart and brought him to accomplish.

It was a daunting task. How can you convince others that what you're doing is from the Lord and that they should join you and Him? No ministry lasts very long without a clear vision that is shared by everyone as they look to serve God. You can't lead without a vision from the Lord and there will be no one to lead until the people hear from God themselves in regard to the work He has set before you.

A real source of frustration for those involved in ministry is when the leader isn't sure what he's doing, where he is going, or has simply failed to share the vision from the Lord with them. This is not so for Nehemiah. He gathered with the people bringing everything he could to lay the work of God before them. He begins by identifying himself with the issues in Jerusalem. He shares their concern rather than bringing reproach upon them for the years of neglect. He might have said, "You all should have built this years ago!" Instead he says: "We are a reproach. Let us go and build."

Timothy was 40 years old when he took the senior pastor position in Ephesus. From prison, Paul wrote his protégé words of direction, comfort, and encouragement. In 1 Timothy 4:12 he said, "Let no one despise your youth, but be an example to the believers in word, in conduct, in love, in spirit, in faith, in purity." Be an example, Timothy! In fact in that entire chapter, Paul speaks almost solely of how Timothy's example would affect and impact the flock.

Nehemiah could have rolled into town and declared, "Look, I'm here from the king. You guys are ridiculously lazy but I am here to fix all that. Now get busy and build the wall. I'll be in the office if you need anything." But that's hardly a good way to lead. Nehemiah instead identifies with God's people. It's hard to hear a Bible teacher suggest we need to pray more but we never find him at any prayer meeting. A true leader should certainly be convinced of the truth he's sharing with others and follow his own counsel as well. If it isn't in your heart, it probably won't be in their hearts either. People know the phonies from the true believers, don't they?

The other thing I want you to notice is Nehemiah's complete lack of pleading or bargaining with the people in the hopes of getting them on board with the vision God had given him. He is willing at every step to let God do the work. Just as he didn't bargain with the king, he doesn't seek to force or manipulate the people to get involved. He believes that if God opens a door, he won't be required to help push the door open.

We have had a policy at our church since we began that we would never go beyond sharing what a need might be in the body and then leave it at that. If a classroom in the Sunday school needs a teacher, we will announce that we could use some more teachers. But if no one shows up, we shut the class down because there's really no sense artificially pumping life into a ministry God is not providing laborers for. After all, we know He builds the church and the gates of hell cannot prevail against it (Matthew 16:18). There is no sense in seeking to accomplish the work of God by beating people over the head with what they should do, appealing to their emotions, or simply pressuring them to respond. God has to work. Unfortunately, there are many who rely on their own ways and they are good at it. They can talk the last five dollars out of your pocket. But I don't want to be good at that. I want to be good at just teaching the Bible and letting God stir hearts.

After all, God doesn't need my help. He doesn't need your help either. I love Nehemiah's approach. He doesn't try to persuade anyone other than to appeal to their spiritual sense. "This is our city," he says. "This is the city God gave us. Our place lies in ruins. I would like to join you and work to get this resolved."

It's interesting how often rewards become an issue in terms of motivation. It's a concept we were introduced to as young children. "Eat all your Brussels sprouts and you'll get dessert. Get more A's than B's and you'll get to go to Disneyland." But notice Nehemiah doesn't say, "A weekend at the Dead Sea for the ones who sign up the most workers!" I think rewards are never the best motivation for serving the Lord because, unfortunately, the rewards have to continue in order for that motivation to continue as well. From what I've learned in the Bible, the best motivation for the saint is God's love. If you love God and feel called by Him to a ministry, nothing and no one will deter you for you love Him so.

We've had people leave our church because I failed to thank them for some service they provided. "Bro, you never thanked me." So I say, "I didn't know you were doing this for me. You should have told me. I thought you were doing this for the Lord and I'm sure He's keeping track." I can't live and die with forgetting to say "thank you," or "you've been a great help," or "aren't you wonderful." I'll wear out and forget someone. If God's called you, then go serve Him and may your reward and your blessing come from Him. That doesn't mean we don't appreciate you, but just watch and see God work. He's the One who should be thanked.

In 1 Samuel 17, when David went out to see his brothers and Goliath was spewing garbage about the God of Israel, David was infuriated. Here is what we read there, in my own words: "Yeah, he's been at this for six weeks," the men of Israel said. "King Saul has said that whoever shuts him up won't have to pay taxes for life, will get a third of the kingdom, and his daughter as a wife. But so far, there have been no takers." "Forget the reward," David said. "This guy's gotta die. He is blaspheming our God. I'll go out and fight him in the name of the Lord and by His strength and power."

> *And I told them of the hand of my God which had been good upon me, and also of the king's words that he had spoken to me. So they said, "Let us rise up and build." Then they set their hands to this good work.*
>
> *–Nehemiah 2:18*

I love verse 18 because Nehemiah was able to testify to them of all that God had done to bring him to this point. In fact, he could tell them to open the doors of the meeting hall and point outside, saying, "See that truck out there filled with wood? That is a present from the king. And there's more where that came from. We've been given everything we need to build the wall of safety and security around our city." Nehemiah was able to present to the people the work that God had already done to encourage them that He was with them and that this was truly His work.

Organizing and leading others is much easier when you've already agonized before God and discovered what He wants to do. Because of his waiting upon God, praying at every step, and planning as he waited, Nehemiah didn't have to walk before this crowd asking them to, "Join me." Instead he could truly say, "Come and join Him. Look what He's been doing. Look at the good hand of God upon us." Planning without agonizing is never good. Agonizing without planning won't work either. But Nehemiah had done both so he could honestly say to the people, "Here's what God has done. Won't you join

Him? Let's build together."

And notice that the overwhelming response of the people was, "Yes, we want to do this." Nehemiah didn't have to pressure anyone. He could just let God be God. Imagine sitting in this meeting hearing Nehemiah begin with, "You're not going to believe how I got here. Seven months ago . . ." and he gave them the whole story of God's marvelous work. Nehemiah got the vision; he shared the vision, and he let God work – and four generations of folks without a wall are now excited to begin to build it again! Get the vision. Share the vision. But as we saw in 2:10 as Nehemiah prepared to come to Jerusalem: expect opposition.

> *But when Sanballat the Horonite, Tobiah the Ammonite official, and Geshem the Arab heard of it, they laughed at us and despised us, and said, "What is this thing that you are doing? Will you rebel against the king?" So I answered them, and said to them, "The God of heaven Himself will prosper us; therefore we His servants will arise and build, but you have no heritage or right or memorial in Jerusalem."*
>
> *–Nehemiah 2:19-20*

We see here that to the original two disturbed officials (2:10), a third one is added, as Geshem joins Sanballat and Tobiah. Three guys isn't a big group yet, but it is a 50 percent increase from when Nehemiah first set out. Eventually there will be armies joining them. The opposition tends to grow as the work of God goes forth. In fact, nearly every step of victory in the book of Nehemiah is followed by a mention of opposition.

For now this small group arrives with scorn and accusations of rebellion. Nehemiah might very well have said, "Well, let me show you the king's letters. Let me bring you a couple of the king's ambassadors that have been riding with me." He had a good case he could have presented to these future enemies of God's work, but he didn't bother. His example is a good one for us because we should never abandon the building for the battle. The work of God should come first. You should never allow yourself to become sidetracked by the opposition because the opposition will come. If you're serving the Lord, the enemy hates it. He doesn't want people to be saved. He doesn't want you to walk with God. He doesn't want you to find the joy of the Lord in serving Him. He's going to take you out if he can. Look at Nehemiah's response: "The Lord is with us. We will serve Him." And he mentions that they have no heritage with us; that's a word from the past. You also have no right; that's present tense. Finally you have no memorial, no future here. The enemy has never found a place in the things of God. He's always the opposition. Nehemiah doesn't preoccupy himself or become distracted by these men and their accusations of rebellion. "Well, we'll just serve the Lord." Learn not to become preoccupied with the taunts of the enemy as you serve God. A few chapters from now, their complaints and threats will be much harder to hear for they will be delivered from the other side of a newly-completed protecting wall.

Chapter 5

Catching The Vision, Letting God Work

Nehemiah 3

Chapter 3 gives us a detailed account of the beginning of the project: who did what, where, how much, if any. Except for a dishonorable mention of a few proud elitists in verse 5, everyone joined in the work. The smallest, the weakest, the richest, the most powerful, the most influential, and the discarded – everyone showed up. So what you find in chapter 3 is a united, excited, warm bond in faith and the progress was almost immediately seen.

I remember many years ago when our church was first planted that because of its small size, whenever any event took place, nearly everyone showed up. We began with less than 100 people. So when we arrived at the school we rented to set up for church services on Sunday morning, it was not unusual to find 50 or more people there to help. They practically just set up their own chair. When it came time for clean up, they stayed and the work was quick and enjoyable. There's something about small that breeds unity. Part of the difficulty of growing is that unity becomes harder to maintain as many more options for involvement are provided. As the church gets larger, it accomplishes more, but at the same time, you need smaller group fellowships within the fellowship to maintain accountability, support, and love on a personal level. I read chapter 3 and think about the days when our church began. Everyone was so willing to do their part. Everyone was so excited about the work God had given us. Everyone was prayerfully reaching out in faith with the good news of Jesus Christ. No one appeared to be jealous of the other and there was tremendous zeal and excitement in the work of the Lord.

As you read the names in this chapter and what they accomplished, you can easily draw the parallel in the way God builds the church. People are called by the Lord and they do their part. They're happy in the place God puts them. They respect what others are doing. There's no friction or disappointment when everything grows from the desire of people to serve the Lord. About a year earlier in this book, there was only one man sitting 700 miles away with a dream in his heart and a vision that God had given him. Now, hundreds or more are building and serving together. What an awesome picture of what God can do if we'll just let Him work.

Why were so many involved? I think you should never separate verse 18 of chapter 2 from all of chapter 3 because, like Nehemiah, the people themselves needed to hear from God. When Nehemiah shared with them the vision God had given him; when he shared his testimony, pointing to what the Lord had done; their hearts were also prompted and stirred. Whenever a work of God is going to be accomplished, chapter 2 has to precede chapter 3. Unless there is a heart that has been touched, a true work of God can't continue. It really can't be any other way; the heart first, then the work.

For years, the Ephesian church had done extremely well. In fact, if you go to Turkey today where the seven remnants of the churches in Revelation are found, the Ephesian ruins and their influence are obviously far greater than those of all of the other churches combined. The work of the Ephesians over the years was phenomenal. The size of the ministry was almost impossible to comprehend. But by the time John sits down to write the book of Revelation and comes to Revelation 2:2-4, it is to the Ephesians that the Lord declares, "I know your works, your labor, your patience, and that you cannot bear those who are evil. And you have tested those who say they are apostles and are not, and have found them liars; and you have persevered and have patience, and have labored for My name's sake and have not become weary. Nevertheless I have this against you, that you have left your first love." Jesus had such accolades for their busy service and much involvement, but then you come to the word "nevertheless" and you wonder, what could be wrong with this? We are the largest church, the most active church, known by all, several gatherings each week, diverse in our outreaches. Yet, "Nevertheless," the Lord declares, "Nevertheless I have this against you, that you have left your first love."

What happened to the Ephesians can so easily happen to any of us. God calls us, begins a work in us, and we go forward fruitfully and joyfully. But over time we lose the connection with God that initially drove us. Eventually, the work remains, churning along with a life of its own, but God is no longer at the center of the work. He has been replaced by sweat, planning, and the confidences of man. Yet notice God is not impressed, nor is He pleased, nor is He moved to help because there's been a separation between the heart and the work. Nehemiah had gathered and shared the vision with the people in chapter 2 and it was they who said, "Let us rise up and work." And they joined the work God was already doing. But for the Ephesians in Revelation, this motive of love had disappeared and been replaced by a very mechanical doing without a relationship and dependency upon Him. God marked the difference. There was still an outward show that continued and impressed man, but the true work of God had stopped. It is as if the Lord said, "I see all that you're doing, but I also see why, and I can't live with the why." This should keep us from pressuring folks into serving the Lord by declaring a need or the benefits of a good work. Rather we should encourage hearts to seek God and keep their relationship with Him as most important so that the works they do will flow from that intimacy with our heavenly Father.

In addition to serving by faith in love, seeing what God had done, the people with Nehemiah also came to serve with the best they had, willing to be used even when not necessarily qualified for the particular task. When Peter wrote his first letter, he said, "If anyone speaks, let him speak as the oracles of God. If anyone ministers, let him do it as with the ability which God supplies, that in all things God may be glorified through Jesus Christ" (1 Peter 4:11). In other words, Peter goes out of his way to say, "Serve to the best of your ability. Give what you can. Do what you're able. And know that to the Lord, that's enough. Bring to the table what God has given you."

Look at our story here. In chapter 3, Nehemiah begins with the priests. Priests are not exactly qualified to build. The only danger in their life was a paper cut or eye strain. "Oh, I can't see. I've been reading all day." But here they are mixing concrete. They are not exactly qualified, but they were out there first, setting the example for others and serving as they could. In fact, most of the laborers in chapter 3 were not serving in the profession or the calling to which they were accustomed – yet everyone was needed. If the wall was to be completed, everyone would need to chip in. Would it have been more logical to have masons and carpenters rather than priests? Of course. But only if you confuse ministry gifts – that which God has specifically enabled or equipped you to do – with the general calling to serve. We're all called to serve. We're all called to give our lives to the Lord and to be available when there is a need. We may have gifts we use regularly, but when the need is presented, we should be willing to serve outside of our expertise trusting God will enable us. That was certainly part of the story here. The folks living in Jerusalem were being robbed and some had been killed. It didn't matter if construction was their calling now; they needed a wall.

Not only did they have a personal conviction and they were willing to serve with what they had, but we find them working together. Jesus had initially sent His apostles out two by two on their first training mission because there is something about working with others that helps us be bold and stay focused. Later, 70 more of His disciples were sent forth, again two by two. The book of Hebrews encourages us to stay in fellowship and not be guilty of "forsaking the assembling of ourselves together" (Hebrews 10:25). We need to be in fellowship because we need the strength that the body brings. The person who asserts that he doesn't need to go to church to be a Christian doesn't understand this. He can probably get by, but he's not going to get by very well. And he'll certainly find himself in direct defiance of God's will for his life.

In Exodus 17, Aaron and Hur held up Moses' arms so that the army of Israel could prevail. In 1 Samuel 14, Jonathan wanted to engage the enemy to see what God wanted to do, so he brought his armor bearer with him so they could be available to God together. Wherever you turn in the Scriptures, working together brought strength and protection. It's one of the many reasons staying plugged into a local body of believers is vital for your spiritual well-being and for your spiritual service. So we are given in this chapter a catalog, a worksheet that includes many of their names and the places they labored. It was quite an organization. Everyone was doing the best they could with a heart for the Lord and His work. Even as the ever-growing naysayers spoke out around them, they put their heads down and worked together. I'm sure the priests ended up with calluses for maybe the first time in their life.

Verse 10 tells us that some of the folks built in front of their own homes. Verses 23, 29, and 30 repeat that as well. There's a good lesson here. Your ministry starts at home, where it matters to you the most. I'm always amazed when I hear those who want to go to the mission field to engage in a spiritual work, a work they have never taken up at home.

The best workers in the nursery are usually the ones who have recently had kids because that's where their heart is. The folks who are part of the jail ministry are oftentimes those who were once incarcerated. They have a heart for the people because they know the needs. Nehemiah understood this, which is why he had the people serve close to their homes, the place of their interests, close to what stirred their hearts and touched their concerns.

Nehemiah made a way for others to catch the vision. He allowed them to serve with what little they had. He had them work together and they began close to home. What great leadership!

Chapter 6

Choose Building Over Battling

Nehemiah 4

Nehemiah's story is a great spiritual analogy of God building your life. You're the temple of the Holy Spirit and God wants to raise you up so that He might use you to bring honor to His name in your culture and your generation.

Here in chapter 4, we learn a couple of important lessons about walking with God that will help us as the enemy seeks to destroy that which God seeks to build. One of the major lessons in the book of Nehemiah is how to serve the Lord in the face of opposition. You would think that after 140 years had passed, the last 60 with a group in the city, that by now anyone showing the slightest interest in rebuilding their walls of security would be greeted and welcomed with open arms. The people should have said, "These guys are troopers. Look at how hard they're trying!" That would have been true in a worldly sense, no doubt, but this is a spiritual work. And because it is God's work and there is an enemy, there's no praise coming. What comes instead is criticism and derision that will eventually lead to persecution, threats, and intimidation. If you learn nothing else from Nehemiah, learn this: If you're going to serve the Lord, the enemy is going to try to stop you anyway he can. In the next few chapters, we will see the growing opposition to the work of God through the enemies of God and His people.

We saw back in 2:10 that initially there were two men deeply disturbed to hear that someone was coming who cared for Jerusalem and its people, and who intended to help and serve them. They had never met Nehemiah and knew nothing of his heart, yet they already opposed him. Who in their right mind would be upset if someone was coming to protect families and children and put a wall around a place that had been overrun for generations? Who would respond, "That's a bad idea. We don't want those kids to feel comfortable walking to school. We don't want those families to feel good sitting out on the patio at night"?

It doesn't make any sense until you realize that when you step out to serve the Lord, you enter a spiritual battle. Even before Nehemiah arrives in town, two men are already against him. It's just a small number for now but it will grow. In fact, the words deeply disturbed (2:10) in Hebrew suggest an overwhelming sadness that grips your outlook. These men were extremely bothered by this potential work.

By application, the single greatest work that you and I have been given by the Lord is to reach the lost. There's really nothing more important. You can do a lot of good things; you can feed the hungry and house the homeless, but if they're not saved when they die, things are only going to get worse for them, not better. The single greatest calling of the church is to go out into the world and preach the gospel of Jesus Christ to every creature. That is the calling for all of us. By example, by word, by struggle – whatever it takes, that's our calling. But the minute we start to do that, we encounter people lost in their sins whose initial response is not welcoming the good news, but resisting it. Some will become deeply disturbed that you are sharing your faith. The battle has begun.

When Paul stood before King Agrippa explaining his conversion on the road outside Damascus, he said: "And when we all had fallen to the ground, I heard a voice speaking to me and saying in the Hebrew language, 'Saul, Saul, why are you persecuting Me? It is hard for you to kick against the goads.' So I said, 'Who are You, Lord?' And He said, 'I am Jesus, whom you are persecuting. But rise and stand on your feet;

for I have appeared to you for this purpose, to make you a minister and a witness both of the things which you have seen and of the things which I will yet reveal to you. I will deliver you from the Jewish people, as well as from the Gentiles, to whom I now send you to open their eyes, in order to turn them from darkness to light, and from the power of Satan to God, that they may receive forgiveness of sins and an inheritance among those who are sanctified by faith in Me'" (Acts 26:14-18). That was Paul's call and that is ours, but therein lies the battle. You will immediately encounter resistance, for man is lost and blind in his sin. Until the light of God's good Word breaks through, the battle rages.

When Paul wrote his second letter to the Corinthians, he talked about the prejudiced attitude of the lost against the people of God. He said in 2 Corinthians 4:3-4, "But even if our gospel is veiled, it is veiled to those who are perishing, whose minds the god of this age has blinded, who do not believe, lest the light of the gospel of the glory of Christ, who is the image of God, should shine on them." So you enter into the battle, don't you? When you step out and begin to serve, the enemy is right there.

Paul told the Ephesians about the spiritual warfare they would face: "Put on the whole armor of God, that you may be able to stand against the wiles of the devil. For we do not wrestle against flesh and blood, but against principalities, against powers, against the rulers of the darkness of this age, against spiritual hosts of wickedness in the heavenly places. Therefore take up the whole armor of God, that you may be able to withstand in the evil day, and having done all, to stand" (Ephesians 6:11-13). It's an important lesson to learn. We are not fighting against people. Your boss is not your enemy, neither is your wife, or your husband, or your neighbor, or the bad driver who cut you off on the freeway. That's the way the world lives. We wrestle against principalities, against powers, against the rulers of darkness in high places, and against the spiritual wickedness of those hosts in heavenly places. We're in a spiritual battle. So as Nehemiah sets off with the blessings of God, the king in his hand, and a song in his heart, an unseen enemy is waiting for him.

Jesus said to the disciples, "If the world hates you, you know that it hated Me before it hated you. If you were of the world, the world would love its own. Yet because you are not of the world, but I chose you out of the world, therefore the world hates you. Remember the word that I said to you, 'A servant is not greater than his master.' If they persecuted Me, they will also persecute you. If they kept My word, they will keep yours also" (John 15:18-20). This was Jesus' warning to His disciples and to us. Step out and opposition will be waiting. You don't have to know them by name, you don't have to be aware of who they are. They may be people you have never met. The nature of the spiritual battle is there will be opposition. Lay your hand to a task for the Lord, open your mouth to share your faith, take a step in God's direction, and you will stir the likes of Tobiah and Sanballat. You may wonder, "What in the world did I do wrong?" The answer is, you haven't done anything wrong. You're doing the right thing and that's why you're having trouble.

So Nehemiah enters into the fray against an opposition whose cause is the sin nature of man. It isn't you, but it's the work of God in you and how you've decided to stand with Him.

Along with this opposition from the natural man lost in his sin, we see another attack upon Nehemiah and his work; that of mockery or ridicule aimed right at you.

In Nehemiah 2:19, we saw the mockery and ridicule begin. By that time Nehemiah had formulated a plan and shared his vision from the Lord with the people. They are enthusiastic and as they begin to step out to do the work of building the wall, they run into this same group who are laughing and despising their work.

Notice the opposition has grown to three. It's only three, but it's a 50 percent increase from 2:10, isn't it? This deeply disturbed, angry little group now begins to laugh and despise even the proposition that these folks were going to go out and do a work for the Lord. They even suggest false motives: "Will you rebel against the king?" Nehemiah knew that wasn't the case. He had just come from the king. All of the supplies he had brought, the king had bought. But that doesn't keep the enemy from accusing you of false motives, or lying, slandering, and mocking you. To his credit, Nehemiah doesn't entertain their complaints or deal with their accusations, but the opposition grows. Here in chapter 4 that opposition continues to rear its ugly head with more and more determination and participation.

> *But it so happened, when Sanballat heard that we were rebuilding the wall, that he was furious and very indignant, and mocked the Jews. And he spoke before his brethren and the army of Samaria, and said, "What are these feeble Jews doing? Will they fortify themselves? Will they offer sacrifices? Will they complete it in a day? Will they revive the stones from the heaps of rubbish – stones that are burned?" Now Tobiah the Ammonite was beside him, and he said, "Whatever they build, if even a fox goes up on it, he will break down their stone wall."*
>
> *–Nehemiah 4:1-3*

I have no doubt that the priests' work in building the wall would produce opportunity to find fault. I don't see the priests as big construction-type guys. It's easy to imagine Tobiah and Sanballat saying, "Look at that wimp trying to swing that hammer. He's going to kill himself!" It is also easy to stop being faithful when criticism from the enemy heads your way. Satan will mock your ideas and question your motives. He'll point out your weaknesses and belittle your accomplishments. He'll seek to sidetrack you, challenge your zeal, and bring up past failure. He's good at slowing you down. But criticism in ministry is always an attempt on the part of the enemy to have you look at things from a human perspective. I think if you set about to work as if everything depended upon you and pray, knowing it all depends upon God, you'll come out on the other side with the right mix of persistence and dependence. God's not looking for talent. He's looking for commitment. He can give you talent. All He needs from you is your faithful, surrendered heart.

Whenever the progress of a work of God increases, so will the attacks of the enemy. Notice that our two friends have found reinforcements and now an entire army stands with them. Their voices are louder. The attacks are stepped up in rhetoric and driven by an ongoing, hateful emotion that so far has failed to derail the work.

Understand that up to this point, they haven't really shown their faces, which is pretty much the way of the enemy. Critics tend to speak, but not to you. They live in the shadows. They mumble behind the scenes. There's an undercurrent of slander, bitterness, and name-calling. They're interested in belittling the work of God and getting you to stop serving. Notice the words they use: feeble, weak, a derogatory term like "you little punk." In other words, "What are you guys trying to pull off here? Are you really going to fortify yourself, protect yourself, and keep yourself safe? I suppose next you're going to turn to your religious ways, stuff that weak people do, and go sacrifice to your God! How long until you are finished?" Mockery!

Tobiah chimes in and begins to criticize how bad the wall looks. "Hey, a little fox jumps on it and it's all going to fall right over." Know that as you go out to serve the Lord, Satan will seek to use criticism to discourage you. He'll portray you as a weak person. "Do you really need Jesus in your life? Do you need to go to church all the time? You can't get it together yourself? What a loser you are!" He will mock you and tell you there's no future in your work, that there's no impact in what you do, no influence, and no lasting fruit.

The media often portrays Christians as being unstable and weak-minded. We're behind the times. We're bigots. We don't believe in a woman's rights. We're prejudiced against homosexuals. We're holier than thou in our attitude toward drinking and premarital sex. The list goes on. We are fodder for the comedians. Start living the Christian life and you may as well paint a target on yourself. That's how Satan works. You begin to serve the Lord and the enemy begins to mock your ideas, question your motives, point out your weaknesses, and highlight your inabilities. He'll laugh at your misdirected zeal and point out everything he can to show how miserable you are. Tobiah is that guy. The enemy seeks to lessen the value of your labors in Him through ridicule.

Look at that wall. Look how it's leaning over. You begin to teach a Bible study because you believe God's called you and only five people show up – and then there are three. And he says to you, "You're not much of a teacher. A couple more weeks of this, you'll be here by yourself…loser." You begin to feed the poor and bring enough food for 10 and 500 show up; all of a sudden, you're inadequate. You begin to step out to support someone and you realize you can't pay for all the things that are necessary though you have a heart to do it, and pretty soon, you're told you're insignificant. The enemy at every step will seek to turn you away. "Why do you witness? Nobody ever gets saved. Why do you bother to pray? Which of your prayers have ever been answered? Do you really think you can make a difference? Look, pal, nobody cares. Wise up. Smell the coffee."

The unfortunate truth is it often works. People hear criticism and they quickly agree and shut down. After all, we hate criticism. Once we get it, we'll do almost anything to rid ourselves of it. If that means shutting my mouth, not living it out, not being true to myself, I'll do it. I won't say anything. I'll just pray in secret. I'll ask God to work. The enemy knows it bothers us and so he resorts to it.

The Bible tells us the fear of man brings a snare (Proverbs 29:25). It sure does. Opposition comes by man's sinful nature and it's usually carried out by mockery. When mockery doesn't work, opposition is ratcheted up. As the work continues, we will find that threats and intimidation become the new operating system for the enemy. Yet here in Nehemiah, through it all, the work of God continues and the Lord protects His people. How did the people keep from giving in to the opposition? They kept their eyes on the Lord.

> *Hear, O our God, for we are despised; turn their reproach on their own heads, and give them as plunder to a land of captivity! Do not cover their iniquity, and do not let their sin be blotted out from before You; for they have provoked You to anger before the builders.*
>
> *–Nehemiah 4:4-5*

I think we know something about this kind of get-even prayer. I remember as a young boy, my sister and I would always fight and one of my favorite lines was, "I am going to tell mom or dad!" It was meant to get the upper hand in the argument. So Nehemiah turns to the Lord, not taking matters into his own hands, but simply placing the situation in His.

I don't know how you handle ridicule, but most people respond in kind. We want to defend ourselves, set the record straight, have the last word, and leave the conversation feeling we have redeemed ourselves. Nehemiah had the king's permission and soldiers in support of him; they might have easily silenced his critics. But Nehemiah doesn't fight back with insults or seek to use other fleshly means to resolve this attack, instead he fights back on his knees. "Look what they're saying about You and Your work, Lord," he prays. It doesn't do any good to fight spiritual battles in the flesh. Nehemiah knows that and instead takes advantage of his access to God in prayer.

Peter wrote to the saints, "For this is commendable, if because of conscience toward God one endures grief, suffering wrongfully. For what credit is it if, when you are beaten for your faults, you take it patiently? But when you do good and suffer, if you take it patiently, this is commendable before God" (1 Peter 2:19-20). You don't need to set every record straight every time for yourself; God has the ability to do that. He knows and is more than able to act on your behalf. He knows the end from the beginning. Nehemiah leaves it with God in prayer and, in so doing, is not sidelined or interrupted in the work at hand.

> *So we built the wall, and the entire wall was joined together up to half its height, for the people had a mind to work.*
>
> *–Nehemiah 4:6*

If you have a mind to work and a heart that's set in prayer before the Lord, opposition will come, but will have little effect on your labor and fruit. It is hard to sidetrack people who aren't easily distracted. It's hard to get someone's attention who's extremely caught up in something else. If you have blinders on and you're looking to the Lord alone, it doesn't matter what is happening around you, for your focus is squarely on Him. Satan's tricks to hinder those who have a mind to work and a heart to pray will fail. Nehemiah and the people with him were preoccupied with the work God had set before them and were making great progress. In fact, the next attack from the enemy comes when the work is half finished and their progress is clearly seen.

> *Now it happened, when Sanballat, Tobiah, the Arabs, the Ammonites, and the Ashdodites heard that the walls of Jerusalem were being restored and the gaps were beginning to be closed, that they became very angry, and all of them conspired together to come and attack Jerusalem and create confusion.*
>
> *–Nehemiah 4:7-8*

The enemy, growing in numbers, gathers again to plan their next move. They will decide to escalate their opposition from simple mockery to much more serious threats of intimidation and violence. Notice in verse 7 how many people have now joined them in opposition to the work of the Lord. At this rate, the critics will soon outnumber the laborers. Their motivation was the evidence of God's blessings upon His people, which is always the case. The enemy becomes angry when the work of God in your life begins to bear fruit. You can certainly expect opposition when you turn to Jesus by faith, stand on His Word, and do what He says. The closer to Him you grow, the more opposition you can expect.

What is interesting about this group standing together in opposition is the fact that historically they didn't get along with each other at all. But now they are brought together as friends against the common enemy of God's people. We see the same thing happening when both Pharisee and Sadducee opposed Jesus. They were theological enemies that both joined with their mutual enemy, the Herodians, and sought to eliminate their common enemy, Jesus. Luke 23:12 tells us the day Jesus was sent to Herod from Pilate was the day Herod and Pilate became friends. Before that, they were rivals.

The Samaritans came from the north of Jerusalem. The Arabians came from the south. The Ammonites were situated to the east, and Philistia, with Ashdod as its capital, was to the west. Enemies and critics surrounded Jerusalem and here we see these enemies joining forces in a plan to create confusion and fear. The king would quickly have forbidden direct war, so they propose to wage a war of terrorism.

It ought to convince you that Satan is not interested in a fair fight. I suspect few of us will ever be asked by God to literally risk our necks for the cause of Christ, though things may change. As long as I've been a Christian, the most threatening thing in America I have ever had to face was ridicule.

Yet we can face persecution in other ways. Your relationship with the Lord and your commitment to Him can certainly be death to your career, your next sale, a friendship you've had for years, or a romance. It can also affect a job advancement or position, possessions, and wealth. There are a lot of things you can lose in the process.

Just as a reminder from verse 6, the opposition always seems far more severe when the work God has set before you is half finished. Half done is a perfect time to become discouraged. Oh, look at all the work we have left to do. But look at all the work that has been done! Why is that when we are half done we feel we have used three-quarters of our energy and strength? I don't know if I can finish now! We will see them saying that very thing in just a few verses.

If your eyes are on the Lord, however, this attack from the enemy will also fail. Did you know that at the height of the Roman persecution of the church in the first few centuries, approximately 10,000 people a day were being killed for their faith, but 50,000 more a day were being saved?

> *Nevertheless we made our prayer to our God, and because of them we set a watch against them day and night.*
>
> *–Nehemiah 4:9*

With the use of the word "we" for the first time, we see the people now following Nehemiah's example and praying. They prayed and then they set a watch. Prayer is never a substitute for being responsible. We pray and we set a watch. Again they turn to prayer because this is a spiritual battle. But they added a second step here as well. "Let us set up a watch for potential attackers." Prayer is never designed to take the place of practical measures that you can responsibly take. Unfortunately, sometimes people over-spiritualize their plight and miss out on all that God would like to do. For example, I spoke to a man out of a job and asked him where he had been looking or applying lately. He said, I have been praying and waiting at home by the phone. I was astounded! "You need to get out there and prayerfully knock on every available door," I told him. How is God going to direct a boat that's docked in the harbor?

We certainly have to seek the Lord in all things, but I think prudent precautions are always our responsibility. Ask the Lord to watch over your house and then lock the door! Prayer is vital, but so is responsible behavior. Notice the word "nevertheless." We're going to do our best, but we're going to keep working. We're counting the cost, we're willing to pay the price, but the work will not stop because of the latest threats! Well, that was true for a time but soon the people stumbled over the mounting pressure of work yet to be done; their own weariness and the threats; and the intimidation and danger brought near by a vocal devoted group of naysayers who sought their destruction.

> *Then Judah said, "The strength of the laborers is failing, and there is so much rubbish that we are not able to build the wall."*
>
> *–Nehemiah 4:10*

Halfway finished and in the face of growing opposition, the people now find themselves absolutely discouraged. It's not easy to maintain your faith when the enemy seems to constantly be on the offensive against your walk with the Lord. Yet that's reality. As long as we are in these bodies serving the Lord, we will be opposed by the enemy of our souls each step of the way. John assures us, "You are of God, little children, and have overcome them, because He who is in you is greater than he who is in the world" (1 John 4:4).

In his second letter to the Corinthians, Paul told them of some of the opposition he had been facing as he preached the gospel, planted churches, and trained others. He wrote, "We are hard pressed on every side, yet not crushed; we are perplexed, but not in despair; persecuted, but not forsaken; struck down, but not destroyed – always carrying about in the body the dying of the Lord Jesus, that the life of Jesus also may be manifested in our body" (2 Corinthians 4:8-10). Paul often faced resistance from the enemy as God worked mightily through his life and we too will face the same. Sometimes, as here, we hit a wall. It had been a hard road to get to a half-built wall. Notice that what the enemy had insinuated about them in verse 2, they now began saying about themselves in verse 10.

It is no coincidence that discouragement overwhelmed them precisely when we read they were halfway done. In anything you do, halfway finished has got to be one of the hardest places to be. It's difficult to be halfway to anywhere, isn't it? I remember when I first started running, I was determined to run 10 miles. I ran 2 laps and then sat and wondered when I would meet the Lord, because I was sure I was dying. Eventually, I got up to running a 10k, 6.2 miles – at which point I said to myself, "Well, that's far enough."

Ever try losing weight and get halfway to your goal only to declare, "I can't do it anymore?" Halfway there brings challenges with it. I think most folks stop loving their car when it's about halfway paid off.

Here the wall was halfway finished, halfway to its designated height, but the next half meant hauling stones and mortar overhead. It was going to be much harder and the same is true in our Christian lives. People get tired of praying, studying, and denying themselves. They argue that the spiritual progress they see is far less than the work they've put in. They get discouraged and want to quit. But if the roots don't go down, the fruit can't come up. That's where these folks were. The wall was half finished and the enemy was right there, trying to let the air out of the balloon.

Back in chapter 2, when Nehemiah said to the people, "Here is what God has already done and here's what He wants to do," the people couldn't join the work fast enough. They were thrilled. Their eyes were on the Lord. But here, their eyes are on the rubbish. Here, the vision which had been for the wall, for their safety, for the protection of their children, and for the witness of the glory of their God had been lost to the rubbish. All they saw was the difficulty ahead of them and the perceived cost in getting it completely finished. Their eyes were no longer on the Lord; they were now on the problem.

New parents are always excited. They've got the nursery prepared. They've got the walls painted. They have everything in place. The little baby comes home and they can't wait to wake him up in the middle of his nap just to look at him. But 50 diapers a day later, this little baby is now only cute when he's asleep. It's the same thing when you get saved. You come to Jesus and begin to learn of His love and you just can't wait to go out and share Him with others. But eventually, the reality of how most people respond to their witness sets in. They're not as welcomed as they thought they would be and they become less motivated to keep trying due to the pain of rejection and ridicule. The hunger they once had to be taught, and to learn, read, and grow in the Lord subsided when reality set in. "Man, this is a lot of work," they say and they lose the vision.

So these folks were being robbed of the joy of the Lord's work in their lives, because the difficulties clouded the importance of what they were doing and hid from their view that which had already been accomplished. Waning faith is a common struggle for Christians as God seeks to build our lives. When the work is half done and the victory half achieved, that's when we often find the greatest difficulties. It's no wonder Paul wrote to the Galatians, "And let us not grow weary while doing good, for in due season we shall reap if we do not lose heart" (Galatians 6:9). You've got to see it through. You've got to press ahead. God has a work to do but the enemy is there trying to stop it.

In the last letter he would write before he was killed, Paul said to a hesitant Timothy in his first senior pastorate, "But you must continue in the things which you have learned and been assured of, knowing from whom you have learned them" (2 Timothy 3:14). In other words, "Timothy, you've got to stick with it. Don't give up now – not when you're halfway home, not when you're halfway there."

God's heart is to build the walls of your life so that He can dwell in you and others can know Him by seeing you. But so often it's discouragement that keeps us from His best and results in loss of vision, loss of confidence, and loss of energy and drive.

> *And our adversaries said, "They will neither know nor see anything, till we come into their midst and kill them and cause the work to cease." So it was, when the Jews who dwelt near them came, that they told us ten times, "From whatever place you turn, they will be upon us."*
> *–Nehemiah 4:11-12*

From sarcasm to jeers to threats of terrorism and attack, the enemy had not taken a day off. In verse 12, we read that it was Nehemiah's own people who had now begun to become the conduits, not of the Word of God and His glorious promises, but of the words of the enemy's threats to their well-being. Notice in particular the words, "So it was, when the Jews who dwelt near them came..." Those repeating and broadcasting these threats to the laborers were the people of God who lived closest to the enemy's camp. They had the least confidence in God, were the first to be influenced by fear, and were the vessels through which the enemy could now destroy the confidence of others. We read here that 10 times they effectively said there is no escape, you will not survive, and we are coming for you! Bad news travels much quicker than good news, doesn't it? They were too far from the center of God's work to share in the joy and thrill of it and far more intimate with the enemy and his ways, than the Lord's.

There are some saints who seem to live closer to the world than they do to the Lord and they can become stumbling blocks to everyone else, conduits by which the enemy can infiltrate. All they can do is point out the difficulties we all face. "Oh, the economy is so bad," they will say, or "Our leaders are awful, how will we ever survive?" They bring the woes of the day, the opinions of others, or the latest poll or editorial to bear on the hearts and hopes of the saints of God. But what we really need to share and hear is what God's Word has to say! Does God worry about a bad economy? I don't think so. Does He need our help to make things better, to turn things around, to give us victory? I don't think so. If He is on the throne, we're fine. We need to be those mouthpieces who bring word from God to the church living in the world, a church that needs to be reached while being opposed by the enemy at every step. We need to speak in His name and for His glory!

> *Therefore I positioned men behind the lower parts of the wall, at the openings; and I set the people according to their families, with their swords, their spears, and their bows. And I looked, and arose and said to the nobles, to the leaders, and to the rest of the people," Do not be afraid of them. Remember the Lord, great and awesome, and fight for your brethren, your sons, your daughters, your wives, and your houses." And it happened, when our enemies heard that it was known to us, and that God had brought their plot to nothing, that all of us returned to the wall, everyone to his work.*
>
> *–Nehemiah 4:13-15*

I love Nehemiah's vision and leadership as he shows it to us here. He positions his workers near their homes so they don't worry while they are away laboring on the wall. He also protects them to the best of his ability. He sets a guard and arms the people. He tells them, "Don't be afraid. Remember your God. He is awesome. He's brought us this far."

There are a couple things that discouragement will usually do to Christians: It'll put you in a place where you isolate yourself from the body and it will cause you to forget God's goodness, power, and past work in your life. Yet there are no promises in the Bible for the security of the loner; our strength is found in the fellowship of the saints.

Nehemiah told them, "We can do our best but after that, we've got to remember God. We can put up the guards. We can arm the people. We can watch the doors. But then we've got to remember that this is a work of God and not of man."

"Why are you cast down, O my soul? And why are you disquieted within me?" asked the psalmist, "Hope in God, for I shall yet praise Him For the help of His countenance" (Psalm 42:5,11; 43:5). I like this kind of self-talk. "What are you doing?" he asks himself. "You've got to trust God. You've got to praise Him for His good work. I know it looks like He's not doing a thing, like you're not being heard, but hang in there. God is faithful and always has been so hope in Him."

It was those who had forgotten who they were serving that were now listening to the lies of the enemy. But at stake in this work of building the wall was everything they counted dear: the safety of their families, their children, their future, the glory of God, and the honor due His name. Everything dear to them depended on the outcome. The same is true in your life; the people you care about need a good witness and need to see the life of someone who's walking with God. No matter what it takes for you to do so, the fruit of it will be worth the effort. Your children need to see an example that they can follow, as does your spouse, your boss, your friends, and your neighbors. The world needs to see a church that believes God enough to walk with Him. To neglect building the wall is to forgo your peace, joy, and hope. In the process of not remembering His ways, the enemy will accomplish his will of killing, stealing, and destroying you and your influence.

Nehemiah said to the people, "We'll do our best, but we can't forget God. He's great and awesome." And God came to their aid. Gloriously, we read here in Nehemiah that all of that discouragement didn't stop the progress. The enemy suffered yet another setback.

> *So it was, from that time on, that half of my servants worked at construction, while the other half held the spears, the shields, the bows, and wore armor; and the leaders were behind all the house of Judah. Those who built on the wall, and those who carried burdens, loaded themselves so that with one hand they worked at construction, and with the other held a weapon. Every one of the builders had his sword girded at his side as he built.*
>
> *–Nehemiah 4:16-18a*

I love this picture because no matter what the discouragement, in the end, the people were not going to stop building to attend to the battle. I hope that's a lesson you take away from these verses. You should never stop the building process of your walk with God to attend to the battle. Paul told the Ephesians, "Finally, my brethren, be strong in the Lord and in the power of His might. Put on the whole armor of God, that you may be able to stand against the wiles of the devil. For we do not wrestle against flesh and blood, but against principalities, against powers, against the rulers of the darkness of this age, against spiritual hosts of wickedness in the heavenly places. Therefore take up the whole armor of God, that you may be able to withstand in the evil day, and having done all, to stand" (Ephesians 6:10-13). He then went on to list the various weapons God gives to us to stand and win the battle (Ephesians 6:14-20): with prayer and supplication, in the Spirit, and with perseverance we continue to walk with Him. We have the sword of the Spirit in hand. We recognize who the enemy is. But know this, building is far more important than battling. Battling comes with the territory but you can't stop the building. Note what Nehemiah does here; he enjoins part of the labor force to stand guard while others keep building. In fact, soon what we build will become our defense from those who would seek to destroy us. If you can only build with one hand, then build with one hand, but we must keep building. If you can only carry half the stuff you used to, that's fine, but keep building. Don't get so caught up in the battle that you stop moving forward.

That can happen so easily. If you ask someone why you haven't seen them in church for some time, they might reply, "Oh, I've really been going through it lately and haven't been coming at all." They put their spiritual well-being aside because life is now too difficult. The battle that should drive them to Jesus now keeps them away.

The walls of our lives have to be built. People have to be saved. You can't quit going to church just because you're having a hard time. You can't stop serving the Lord just because life has become difficult. Build, man! That's what we're called to do, not to get so sidetracked with battling that we never get anything done. If Satan can reduce you to just fighting battles, you'll neglect to witness to lost souls. You'll neglect your spiritual life, your prayer life, your Bible study, and your church life, and then the enemy wins. The work won't continue. It's the building that God's interested in. You cannot leave the building for the battle.

John Wesley went to jail five times for preaching and the minute he was released, he returned to preaching Jesus. Because of him, the Methodist revival of his day spread like wildfire. Tens of thousands of people were saved because one man would not stop building to attend to the battle. The battles certainly came his way, but it was the building he was interested in.

> *And the one who sounded the trumpet was beside me. Then I said to the nobles, the rulers, and the rest of the people, "The work is great and extensive, and we are separated far from one another on the wall. Wherever you hear the sound of the trumpet, rally to us there. Our God will fight for us." So we labored in the work, and half of the men held the spears from daybreak until the stars appeared. At the same time I also said to the*

people, "Let each man and his servant stay at night in Jerusalem, that they may be our guard by night and a working party by day." So neither I, my brethren, my servants, nor the men of the guard who followed me took off our clothes, except that everyone took them off for washing.

–Nehemiah 4:18b-23

Nehemiah said, "We're all going to work in our assigned areas, but if there's trouble, a trumpet will sound and we'll run and stand together, and watch God work. These are difficult times and we need to make sacrifices." Then he took the final practical step of moving many of the laborers into town. They didn't go home at night. They stayed to stand guard, they gave it their all.

Are you discouraged? Be encouraged that the work is far too important to stop now! Half done means only this: we're half done. Let's not rest until we're finished! As Paul said in Philippians 1:6, "being confident of this very thing, that He who has begun a good work in you will complete it until the day of Jesus Christ." He won't quit on you when you are halfway home! God makes no provision for you being on your own. But if you assemble and serve together, the walls will go up, the enemy won't have a way in, and God will be glorified. It will take a real commitment, just as we see here with the saints on the wall.

Chapter 7

Attacks From Within, Leading By Example

Nehemiah 5

In chapter 5, Nehemiah faces the next onslaught from an enemy that doesn't give up. By the middle of chapter 6, the wall will indeed be finished and afford the saints great protection. Here in chapter 5, he turns to yet another attack, one that almost brings the work to a complete standstill. Up until this point, every attack had come from without in the form of ridicule, sarcasm, and even serious threats of violence, but now the enemy takes a new tact. This time the attack comes from within in the form of internal dissension, hatred, and strife in the camp that caused the people to start choosing sides and drawing lines. It slowed the work they should have been doing to a crawl. Satan was warming up for a victory lap. "I have them now," he thought.

There's an old saying that we have met the enemy and he is us, but that shouldn't be so for the people of God. It is easy to lose sight sometimes of the fact that the body of Christ in God's view is one body. We are family in this work of growing in Him and reaching this lost world together. So the enemy sets his sights on that unity and that work. He seeks to stir up internal dissension, remaining neutral and feeding both sides plenty of deadly ammunition.

Paul wrote to the Galatians, "For you, brethren, have been called to liberty; only do not use liberty as an opportunity for the flesh, but through love serve one another. For all the law is fulfilled in one word, even in this: 'You shall love your neighbor as yourself.' But if you bite and devour one another, beware lest you be consumed by one another!" (Galatians 5:13-15). Paul was aware of and warned often of how the enemy works. If he can't get you from without – through the pressure of the world's system, through the attacks of those who hate you and the God you serve – he will try and come at you from within – through the people who sit in your row at church or work in ministry beside you. There's always a way in or so he thinks.

One of the most effective works of the enemy is to sow discord. Revelation 12:10 tell us that Satan sits before the Lord's throne night and day to accuse you before your God of your failures, your sins, inconsistencies, etc. He enjoys nothing more than that. So when we start doing that with each other, we become a tool for the enemy. Often we find folks having difficulty in their service for the Lord or, if you want to stay with the analogy, having difficulty building the walls of their lives spiritually because someone has embittered them, failed them, hurt them, sinned against them, or stolen their joy.

Solomon wrote in Proverbs 6:16-19: "These six things the LORD hates, Yes, seven are an abomination to Him: A proud look, A lying tongue, Hands that shed innocent blood, A heart that devises wicked plans, Feet that are swift in running to evil, A false witness who speaks lies, And one who sows discord among brethren." In Hebrew grammar, the method of putting an exclamation point behind anything is to use ascending numbers as here: five, no six, no seven. The last one on Solomon's list is: he who sows discord among the brethren, the divider, the backbiter, the one who makes life difficult for others. Be careful as God works in your life that the enemy's ploy of internal dissension doesn't stumble you and stop the Lord's work. Whether it's questioning someone's motives or grumbling about their methods, disagreeing with a decision of an overseer, or complaining about someone's mannerisms, none of those things come from God's throne. You don't want to become the enemy's pawn. You instead want to be the one who is used by the Lord to continue the work. This was exactly what the laborers with Nehemiah were now facing as they sought to finish the wall of protection around the city of God.

> *And there was a great outcry of the people and their wives against their Jewish brethren. For there were those who said, "We, our sons, and our daughters are many; therefore let us get grain, that we may eat and live." There were also some who said, "We have mortgaged our lands and vineyards and houses, that we might buy grain because of the famine." There were also those who said, "We have borrowed money for the king's tax on our lands and vineyards. Yet now our flesh is as the flesh of our brethren, our children as their children; and indeed we are forcing our sons and our daughters to be slaves, and some of our daughters have been brought into slavery. It is not in our power to redeem them, for other men have our lands and vineyards." And I became very angry when I heard their outcry and these words.*
>
> *–Nehemiah 5:1-6*

We learn here that the wall was being built during a time of tremendous national crisis. It is always true that the church is to flourish while the world lies under pressure in great darkness. Yet, the people of God do not escape the difficulty found in the world. In fact, it placed a great strain upon them as well. Verse 2 tells us there were large families who had difficulty feeding everyone. Times were desperate. The property owners had mortgaged their lands not to get ahead, but to simply eat and survive. The taxes of Artaxerxes, Nehemiah's boss, in verse 4 had placed even greater burdens upon the people. Some of the folks had quit going to work, but had come to live in town to be protection for the folks who were building. They were setting aside their own needs for the well-being of the rest.

As a result, the people were being enslaved for their inability to pay, a typical Old Testament practice in the world. Lands were being seized and the kids were being sold into slavery so they could pay the debts. If this situation wasn't hopeless enough as the people were seeking to walk with God, the worst thing was, according to verse 1, this was coming from their brethren, from the saints. The pressure and the selling of the children, the loans at the high rates, the mortgages with the oppressive terms, and the injustice for the sake of gain were being pursued by their brethren. The result was everyone hated one another, mistrusted one another, and accused one another. Life drained out of the work of God.

Consider what we see here. The people had been greatly united when the work of God was set before them and they realized He was with them. They had even been willing to risk their very lives in their service to God. But being taken advantage of by their own brothers was more than they could handle.

Every division in the body of Christ is caused by someone looking out only for himself. It doesn't really matter what that is. Whether it's power, the flesh, gain, or pride, division comes when someone is interested in himself more than he's interested in others or the things of God. A true disciple of Jesus will seek to avoid that. Jesus said, "Whoever desires to come after Me, let him deny himself, and take up his cross, and follow Me" (Mark 8:34b). God's solution for every divisive issue is to deny yourself and seek His glory.

The enemy had not been able to stop the work of God through ridicule and threat. However, he was almost able to accomplish it through the selfish pursuit of the flesh of just a few, and the result was division and outrage. If we translate this situation to practical living, someone might have said, "I'm leaving that church. I'll find another place to go." I'm amazed how often the solution for conflict with others is to simply go somewhere else. Let me just save you a trip: You're going to find the same problems anywhere you go, because the church is filled with sinful people getting saved. It's not going to change from one place to the next. The solution isn't to run and hide. Yes, run away if there is ongoing sin, false doctrine, or ungodly practices, but under most circumstances, deal with it, work it out, die to self, walk in love, and let God be God. It'll suit you far better in the long run than hightailing it somewhere else.

Here, there really wasn't anywhere for these people to run. They had to face it and deal with it. Nehemiah was furious and I can understand that. According to the Old Testament law for the Jews, they weren't to do any of these things to each other; they were one people. There was very clear direction from God's Word that they were to act differently. In fact, the best protection you and I have, as Christians, from the enemy and his wicked plans is to simply obey the Scriptures. That's our protection. God says, "Go this way." Alright, I'll go that way and on that path. The enemy can't pursue us there; he's against the things of God. If you're walking with God, you're safe. But if you start saying, "Well, that's what the Lord says, but I think differently," then you put a bull's-eye right on your back. You say to the devil, "Shoot me. I'm right here." This is because you've deviated from the Scriptures.

Nehemiah was furious because the people had set aside the clear counsel of God. Though God had been doing this wonderful work, the enemy found an open door through the disobedience of some. Subterfuge, underhanded dealing, and wickedness would begin to work. The Lord had said through Moses in Exodus 22:25, "If you lend money to any of My people who are poor among you, you shall not be like a moneylender to him; you shall not charge him interest." Deuteronomy 23:19-20 says, "You shall not charge interest to your brother–interest on money or food or anything that is lent out at interest. To a foreigner you may charge interest, but to your brother you shall not charge interest, that the LORD your God may bless you in all to which you set your hand in the land which you are entering to possess." And in Leviticus 25:35-37, it says "If one of your brethren becomes poor, and falls into poverty among you, then you shall help him, like a stranger or a sojourner, that he may live with you. Take no usury or interest from him; but fear your God, that your brother may live with you. You shall not lend him your money for usury, nor lend him your food at a profit."

It couldn't have been any clearer; the Scriptures are straightforward and Nehemiah was furious because these folks had willfully ignored and disobeyed God. This wonderful work, which was more than halfway done, was going to be absolutely stopped again; not because there was an enemy outside laughing, but because there was an enemy within who had succeeded in having some use and abuse one another.

We have the same direction in the New Testament for fellowship among the saints. Wherever you turn, you read, "Be kind to one another. Be tenderhearted. Forgive one another as God has in Christ forgiven you. Be imitators of God. Be as His dear children. Esteem others better than yourself. Provoke one another to love and good works." What a distinction from those who would sow discord and serve as tools of the enemy, pursuing self in defiance of God's Word. Be assured, if you're going to walk with God, if the enemy can't get you from without, he'll try and discourage you from within. That is life in the body.

> *After serious thought, I rebuked the nobles and rulers, and said to them, "Each of you is exacting usury from his brother." So I called a great assembly against them. And I said to them, "According to our ability we have redeemed our Jewish brethren who were sold to the nations. Now indeed, will you even sell your brethren? Or should they be sold to us?" Then they were silenced and found nothing to say. Then I said, "What you are doing is not good. Should you not walk in the fear of our God because of the reproach of the nations, our enemies?"*
>
> *–Nehemiah 5:7-9*

I like that rather than going off half-cocked in anger, Nehemiah first gives the problem some serious thought. That's a great leadership trait, isn't it? He is slow to anger, slow to speak, and quick to hear. I like Nehemiah's willingness to put it all on the line to do the right thing because the folks he calls out in public are the rich, the wealthy, the influential, the powerful, and probably the wrong guys to turn on in a rebuilding effort. These were probably the men who had the most influence when it came to building, machinery, equipment, and resources. However, Nehemiah was interested in doing what God wanted so that His blessing might remain upon them. He was not interested at all in depending upon powerful men to keep God's work moving forward.

I'm constantly encouraged that you don't need to compromise your faith by outwardly pleasing people just because they may help you in the short term. That's not the way God works. In the end, God has to be pleased and relied upon. If you'll put Him first, you'll be far better off than trusting in someone else, because trusting in someone other than God is what the Bible calls idolatry, not faith.

So Nehemiah sought to know God's heart. Paul had the same attitude as he came to Thessalonica with the gospel so many years later, saying "But as we have been approved by God to be entrusted with the gospel, even so we speak, not as pleasing men, but God who tests our hearts. For neither at any time did we use flattering words, as you know, nor a cloak for covetousness--God is witness. Nor did we seek glory from men, either from you or from others, when we might have made demands as apostles of Christ. But we were gentle among you, just as a nursing mother cherishes her own children" (1 Thessalonians 2:4-7). So often we are tempted to only please people. But I think the courage of any leader is to stick with God's ways at all costs, though from a worldly perspective it was bad strategy to confront these high profile people. They could have provided the work with great support, but they also could have caused him the most trouble. Either way,

Nehemiah couldn't have cared less. Dependence on the Lord was his outlook of faith.

I admire that very much. The difficult part of leading in this way is the risk you run of alienating people. They're no longer going to be your friends because you've taken a stand to please the Lord. I think of Paul standing up to Peter in Galatians. Peter had experienced the freedom of God's grace, but he had come from the Jerusalem church, which had a much harder time accepting it. When Peter got away from Jerusalem, he'd fellowship and eat with Gentiles until he heard some folks from the Jerusalem church were coming. Then he quickly moved over to the kosher side of the picnic. Paul called him out on it, "Hey, Peter!" he said. "Your hot dog order is getting cold!" For the sake of the gospel, Paul put Peter in his place (Galatians 2:11-14).

I love Nehemiah's willingness to do the same thing, to stand before the people and say, "This is not right. This is sin. You can't do this." He didn't just call them out, he also gave them a solution.

> *"I also, with my brethren and my servants, am lending them money and grain. Please, let us stop this usury!"*
> *–Nehemiah 5:10*

Nehemiah had been helping others in their distress, as had his servants, but to help them, not make use of them for profit. So his counsel is to stop this usury!

The first step to take when you find yourself in a place God doesn't want you is simple: stop it. This has shortened my counseling hours considerably. People come in and say, "You know what I've been doing . . ." and I say, "Stop doing that."

When caught in sin, most people feel bad, but only a few feel bad enough to stop it! Or they'll say, "How am I supposed to quit?" Instead of determining in their hearts to obey, they turn to some system: 10 methods, eight steps, and seven ways to accomplish victory, none of them addressing obedience, faith, and God's power to deliver us from sin. They may even seek to excuse their behavior by saying, "Well, you know, I'm emotionally scarred. It's my psychological bent. My father was an alcoholic, too." Yeah, just stop it. We need to hate what God hates, let God work, and stop it now.

> *"Restore now to them, even this day, their lands, their vineyards, their olive groves, and their houses, also a hundredth of the money and the grain, the new wine and the oil, that you have charged them."*
>
> *–Nehemiah 5:11*

The next step to take when you seek to go back to God's ways is to make things right, restore what was lost, provide restitution, give back what you've stolen. Don't just say you're sorry, rather fix it. The trespass offering of the Old Testament required sacrifice, confession of sin, and restitution of 120 percent of what was taken, lost, etc.

One final important step in restoration back to God's ways is to do it now, or as Nehemiah said, "even this day." You can't stop sinning gradually. There's no taking baby steps back to Jesus. Now is the day of salvation, Paul declared in 2 Corinthians 6:2. "Choose for yourselves this day whom you will serve," Joshua cried in Joshua 24:15. If you put off what God speaks to you until a later day, the sands of time will begin to dull the sharp edges of God's reproof and you may end up ignoring His Word completely.

To not act immediately when God has spoken to us is a constant danger for the saint. God speaks, the light is on, the door is open, the Spirit is moving – but if you procrastinate and move out from under the light you can soon lose the conviction and concern that God had brought to your heart. So, "pay it back today," Nehemiah says.

I can envision these wealthy businessmen walking from tent to tent returning funds to the poor. It must have been humiliating for them, but it was healing for the body and the work of God. Nehemiah continues to be a leader others could follow as he followed the Lord. It brought life to the people again. Repentance, after all, is not a philosophy; it's an attitude and an action.

> *So they said, "We will restore it, and will require nothing from them; we will do as you say." Then I called the priests, and required an oath from them that they would do according to this promise.*
>
> *–Nehemiah 5:12*

"We'll give the money back," the men said. "I don't trust you carnal guys very much right now," Nehemiah said. "Let's bring a priest here and you can swear to God about your promise to restore all." I love this! Nehemiah's point is that unless you find yourself accountable to the Lord, even the call of others to repent or forgive won't keep you going. If God's not involved, it's not going to last. Stop and restore. Do it today and make sure you know God's watching.

> *Then I shook out the fold of my garment and said, "So may God shake out each man from his house, and from his property, who does not perform this promise. Even thus may he be shaken out and emptied." And all the assembly said, "Amen!" and praised the LORD. Then the people did according to this promise.*
>
> *–Nehemiah 5:13*

Nehemiah publicly asked God to deal with those who might have another trick up their sleeves, but their words were sincere and everyone was blessed. Obedience brought joy and doing right brought restoration; sin was defeated, unity was restored, and the people went back to work. In fact, aside from an attack on Nehemiah personally between here and the end of chapter 6, the people are free to finish the work that God had set before them.

Moreover, from the time that I was appointed to be their governor in the land of Judah, from the twentieth year until the thirty-second year of King Artaxerxes, twelve years, neither I nor my brothers ate the governor's provisions.

–Nehemiah 5:14

Nehemiah, in the concluding verses of this chapter, beginning here in verse 14, will set before us some valuable insights regarding personal integrity, a testimony to the private affairs of a man that God has greatly used. What is he doing when no one sees? The context of the verses begins with the word "moreover," attaching whatever follows to what has gone before. There had been a famine. There was tremendous taxation. The people were impoverished and yet some of the wealthy Jews began to gouge the people they were supposed to stand alongside as family. They raised taxes. They took land in exchange for non-payment. They enslaved the children of those in debt. Nehemiah had enough.

Because the subject came up, Nehemiah also felt he had to distinguish himself from these wicked, selfish nobles and say to the people, "I haven't been doing those kinds of things." In the process, we're given an inside look at Nehemiah's personal life that we might otherwise rarely see.

Nehemiah 5:14-19 becomes a wonderful example of the kind of leadership God is looking for in the church. The Scottish writer, Thomas Carlisle wrote, "Adversity is a painful trial we have to endure. There's only one thing worse than adversity – advancement." Few, even in the Bible, seem to do well living in the lap of luxury, having great power, and still maintaining their spiritual balance. Few folks can morally, emotionally, and spiritually remain on the high ground while the best the world has to offer is laid at their feet. Few people can handle promotion and still bring God the glory He deserves.

However, some can. One who would, Asaph, was a

very wealthy man who wrote 12 psalms. He had his head and his heart together before the Lord. He wrote in Psalm 75:5-7, "Do not lift up your horn on high; Do not speak with a stiff neck. For exaltation comes neither from the east Nor from the west nor from the south. But God is the Judge: He puts down one, And exalts another." The word horn is a Hebrew word that means power, authority, or influence. He advised not to go and push yourself forward. Don't speak with a stiff neck because your exaltation does not come from the east or from the west or from the south. It comes from the Lord. In other words, God has placed you in the position you have acquired and the place you find yourself as a believer. He declared God would judge and put down one while exalting another. Tooting your own horn is a foolish practice; we should rather exalt God and worship Him!

The world, of course, sees advancement and promotion far differently. They see it as a birthright for some and as great luck for others. Some take credit for their success because of their shrewdness or hard work. Yet from the Lord's standpoint, it is a position God gives to some for the sake of serving Him. David goes from tending sheep to being the king over the greatest nation upon the face of the earth at the time. Joseph goes from being enslaved and then falsely imprisoned to overnight becoming the prince of a world governing empire. Daniel went from being a prisoner of war taken in the first wave of Babylonian occupation to becoming the vice president to two world-governing empires by the hand of God. Amos graduated from fig-picker school and became the national spokesman for years to bear God's Word to the people. Each of them handled their exalted positions with grace and faith. As a result, they found tremendous success, never once setting God aside or compromising their relationship with Him for the sake of gain. So Nehemiah gives us an insight into his own life in comparison to these men he had called out publicly. They're vital issues for us to know and you can place them under the title: Leading By Example.

In chapter 2, we read that it was in the 20th year of Artaxerxes' reign that Nehemiah had asked the king for permission to begin the building project in Jerusalem. Here we read that Nehemiah was appointed governor of Judah in that same 20th year. His appointment could have been part of a package deal by Artaxerxes. "I'll let you go build the wall, but while you're there, I want you to represent the kingdom."

I don't know if Nehemiah felt he could be a governor, but then again he wasn't a wall-builder, either. Yet, whatever he was going to do, he was going to be sure he used his position to honor the Lord.

The apostle Stephen rose to a place of great service to the Lord through being faithful in the little things. He waited tables before he began to preach. Moses watched sheep before he led God's people. And God used these men mightily because, although they were willing to go forward to a place of power and privilege, they didn't use their position for themselves. Instead, they sacrificed greatly in their position and set self aside. That is why Nehemiah was able to say, "For the last 12 years, I haven't used any of the benefits I've been given for personal gain – not for myself, not for my family. I served in such a way that the Lord would be honored."

The governor's income came through taxation of the people. Under the law, Nehemiah could have set the taxes at any rate he wanted. He had a tax-free status with the king. He had an expense account and unlimited privileges. But Nehemiah held it all at arm's length, for it is an area where the enemy can undermine any spiritual work. If you preach spiritual values and heavenly rewards but live a carnal life, it really doesn't matter if the message you preach is right, because no one's listening anymore. You have undermined your testimony and witness by your very behavior.

We hear of politicians getting on planes to take their kids for a haircut 6,000 miles away using the government's planes and money. We're shocked, as if somehow we would never do that. You know why you would never do that? Because you don't have a plane! Temptation really isn't a temptation until there's an opportunity. Promotion often brings the opportunity. That is why using our attained position for the Lord's glory is absolutely essential.

The disciples spent three-and-a-half years arguing about greatness behind Jesus' back. You never hear them saying, "I want to be a better servant. I'm going to serve more than you." No, they said, "I'm going to get a title better than yours and a corner office bigger than yours. I'm going to have more access to Jesus than you are. I'm going to sit right next to Him when He takes over." The disciples struggled for power, while Jesus had come to lay down His life for the sins of the world.

The world hates corruption. Unbelievers hate corruption. The politician stands and says, "We are broke and I'm only taking a 22 percent raise." It drives people crazy, but it's life in the world, life without God, and power for self. So you shouldn't be surprised. Yet, it becomes a tragedy when you find it among God's people. God hates it. It robs us of our distinction in Him and it reveals the true condition of our heart. Nehemiah begins by saying of himself, "I have set aside the privilege of my office for the sake of my service. I'll hold my example up for anyone to see. You're welcome to follow it, and not just me, but my staff as well. We have done so from day one!"

> *But the former governors who were before me laid burdens on the people, and took from them bread and wine, besides forty shekels of silver. Yes, even their servants bore rule over the people, but I did not do so, because of the fear of God.*
>
> *–Nehemiah 5:15*

Nehemiah could have followed the example and the long history of all of the governors who went before him. They enriched themselves by overtaxing the people. They changed the rates to match their lifestyles. They demanded things they couldn't resist. Nehemiah might well have said, "Hey, this is the way it's always been. I didn't write the rules. I'm just playing along with them." But he didn't. He chose instead to be above reproach, to give the enemy no foothold. For him promotion brought an opportunity to make a difference, to bring change, to shine as God's representative, to walk the walk.

"I know how to be in charge and I know how to be under authority," the centurion had said to Jesus in Matthew 8, a statement of faith that acknowledged Jesus was God. That's how Nehemiah felt as well. He was a good leader because he was first under the authority of God; he feared the Lord.

In 1 Kings 12, when Solomon's son, Rehoboam, came to the throne, the old-timers who were around in his father's administration said, "You should back off on the taxes. The people are dying under the weight. Your father liked to build and he didn't care who it hurt. You would do the people a great service by making it easier for them." But Rehoboam's young friends said, "No way. In fact, say to the people, 'My father had his thumb on you. But I'm going to put my knee in your back.'" Rehoboam heeded the counsel of his young, inexperienced, self-driven friends. Soon the nation split in two and he lost his kingdom.

There were other men, like Joseph, who had great authority and used their position to serve the Lord no matter where they found themselves. There was never a thought of personal gain for Joseph. He wasn't driven by self-interest and yet he was a very wealthy man; so were Abraham, David, and many others. They had wealth but their wealth didn't have them, so God was able to use them from that place of prosperity. Nehemiah is a striking example of that kind of useful man.

"Former governors did this but I did not do so," Nehemiah said. I think that's something that you and I, as Christians, need to say more often. I can't tell you how many times I've heard the argument, "That's the way it's always been done." But if you're in a position to change the situation for good, change it, and refuse to follow the custom. You don't have to live by the status quo. Nehemiah sought what God would have wanted. He only wanted to please his Lord. He broke the mold and restored confidence in government. He was an awesome witness in his day!

It's essential for a leader in the church to set the tone instead of following the crowd. Following the crowd is easy until the crowd changes its mind. God doesn't change; so let His Word set the standard. If something matters to God, make sure it matters to you and to those under you. David wrote, "Who may ascend into the hill of the LORD? Or who may stand in His holy place? He who has clean hands and a pure heart, Who has not lifted up his soul to an idol, Nor sworn deceitfully. He shall receive blessing from the LORD, And righteousness from the God of his salvation" (Psalm 24:3-5).

If we live for Him and we let His Word be the standard for us to follow, we're going to be free from the "everybody's doing it" argument and we're going to be found in a place where we're pleasing the Lord. Jesus said in John 14:23, "If anyone loves Me, he will keep My word; and My Father will love him and, We will come to him and make Our home with Him." The former governors justified the wicked oppression of the people by sharing the wealth. Yes, we're gouging, but we're not keeping it all for ourselves. We're giving some to our buddies. Even the servants got to rule over the people; graft set in and there was privilege at all levels. Not Nehemiah, no way. He used his position of promotion to bring change that honored God. How good is that?

> *Indeed, I also continued the work on this wall, and we did not buy any land. All my servants were gathered there for the work.*
>
> *–Nehemiah 5:16*

I suspect that land in Jerusalem was pretty cheap before the wall was up. The minute the city was secure, the land was worth a lot of money and Nehemiah knew it was coming. He had "insider" information. So if he had wanted to make a fortune for himself, this was the way to do it. He could have had an expansionist kind of philosophy and while folks were building on the front end, he could have been buying on the back end and no one could have stopped him. But that wasn't his interest. He kept his focus and not only did he stay on track, but his servants did as well. Nehemiah had great influence. He led by example. In fact, he added that all his staff also did not buy any land and everyone had a singular focus, a singular purpose, they were there to do the work of building the wall and providing security for God's people.

The world expects to see us live different lives and there is this interesting dichotomy for Christians who are anxious to prove to the world that their belief system is different. We want to be as different as chalk is from cheese. Yet when it comes to our behavior, somehow we desire to be just like the world. We want to fit right in. We want our beliefs to be absolutely, radically distinct, but our behavior to be absolutely non-distinct. That will never work. We're going to have to practice what we preach. We're going to have to live what God speaks to us about. We can't fit in. The world has to see the joy of the Lord in God's people as it looks for honest men and women in power; men like Nehemiah who wouldn't profiteer in the work he'd been given and not allow anyone around him to do it either. To God be the glory.

Promotion brings great accountability. It brings much privilege that can be abused, but it also brings the opportunity to change things for God's glory, if a leader will just take a narrow view of his work and be the model others can follow.

> *And at my table were one hundred and fifty Jews and rulers, besides those who came to us from the nations around us. Now that which was prepared daily was one ox and six choice sheep. Also fowl were prepared for me, and once every ten days an abundance of all kinds*

> *of wine. Yet in spite of this I did not demand the governor's provisions, because the bondage was heavy on this people.*
>
> *–Nehemiah 5:17-18*

Promotion that God can use often comes at a price. Nehemiah found himself personally caring for 150 people each day. I think he brings this up because, after putting some guys in their place for cheating others, he didn't want anyone to think for five minutes that he was only talking a good game, but not living it. Nehemiah put his money where his mouth was, where his Lord was. Every day, 150 folks sat down to eat with him and he picked up the tab. It couldn't have been easy but he did all he could at great personal expense. The alternative would have been to create a governor's salary by placing even higher taxes upon the people, which he was unwilling to do. He wouldn't be a stumbling block. His policies would support what God was doing. His faith would be set on display and his relationship with God translated into loving kindness and self-sacrifice.

> *Remember me, my God, for good, according to all that I have done for this people.*
>
> *–Nehemiah 5:19*

"God, You keep track of the sacrifices I'm making," Nehemiah prayed. "I just want You to be happy." Nehemiah kept his eye on the ball. He had the long view. The folks who were getting rich and oppressing others were looking at what they could get tomorrow and next week. Nehemiah looked all the way to the end and said, "God, You remember."

What a great picture! I read the story of a young violinist who gave his first recital at Carnegie Hall at the age of 14. He played a very difficult piece so well that when he was done, the crowd gave him a standing ovation. But the young protégé just looked to the balcony. He was looking for the approval of his teacher. So are we! People can cheer if they like, but I want to see God smile. I want to hear Him say, "Well done. Thumbs up. Way to go. Good call. Right choice." That's all Nehemiah desired as well.

I doubt Nehemiah felt comfortable drawing attention to the number of individuals he was feeding out of his own pocket each day. Yet, it teaches us that if we want to serve and be promoted to the place of the greatest usefulness in the kingdom of God, we are going to have to live a life above reproach, focused on pleasing God alone, even when it costs us. You're going to be called to set standards for others to follow rather than allowing others to set the standards for you.

So who's following you? And what does it cost you? What if the whole church was just like you? What if the spiritual life of everyone in the body was just like yours? Would it be a better place, a more effective witness? Or would we have to close studies because no one was showing up? Would we be sending out more missionaries or would we be bringing them home because we couldn't support them?

"Imitate me, just as I also imitate Christ," Paul told the Corinthians (1 Corinthians 11:1). Nehemiah could say it as well, "Come and do like me." Can you say that? Be like Paul; be like Nehemiah. Invest yourself and be a witness. Serve the Lord.

Chapter 8

Ministry Requires Perseverance

Nehemiah 6

In chapter 6, we come to the final step of the first part of Nehemiah's work and journey, that of finishing the wall. We also come to the last ditch effort on Satan's part to stop this work, now going after Nehemiah himself. Whether the enemy attacks from without or from within, life in the world serving the Lord will be hard. Attempting to put the Lord first in everything you do is the best life you could live, but it isn't the easiest one. I realized the other day that I've been saved over 40 years. I can't say that it has gotten easier, but it has continued daily to get better and better. The challenges are different now. My faith in His Word is established, my worries about my salvation are gone, and my desire for things of this world has lessened. Yet, I see sin and rebellion still rearing their ugly head in my life. The constant battle to surrender all requires what Paul determined to do in his own life, as he told the Philippians (Philippians 3:13-14). Yet, just as often, I feel like the disciples of Jesus in Luke 17:5 as they responded to His teaching that unlimited forgiveness should be offered to our enemies: "And the apostles said to the Lord, 'Increase our faith.'" I can relate to that prayer! Whether the enemy's attacks come from without or from within, whether you, your work, your family, or your friends are his focus, faith in God and His Word and work are essential. Our faith in Him can grow as we stay the course (Romans 10:17). Jesus told us that in the world we would have tribulation (John 16:33) and here the enemy takes one last swing at God's work, this time directly at Nehemiah. His aim now is to topple the work from the top, going after Nehemiah himself.

"Well done, good and faithful servant," said the master in Jesus' parable from Matthew 25. "You were faithful over a few things, I will make you ruler of many things. Enter into the joy of your lord" (Matthew 25:21). The reward for faithfulness is more work, more opportunity, and more responsibility. At each turn and with each new open door, the enemy awaits to oppose and hinder the work of God in and through your life.

Faith in God is certainly at the hub of our walk with God. Unfortunately for many Christians, the subject of faith is mostly viewed in terms of receiving. "Well, we just believed the Lord and here's what He did for us ..." But that's not really biblical faith at its core. By definition, biblical faith refers to the time when I wait upon God, when I believe He will do as He has said, and yet see none of it. In Hebrews 11:1, Paul wrote, "Now faith is the substance of things hoped for, the evidence of things not seen." James would add that faith without works is dead faith (James 2:17). So as I believe God, I have to live in a way that says to everyone who knows me, "I believe God will do all He has said He will do – even though I might not see it yet."

Paul wrote to the Romans, "For we were saved in this hope, but hope that is seen is not hope; for why does one still hope for what he sees? But if we hope for what we do not see, we eagerly wait for it with perseverance" (Romans 8:24-25). Faith is no longer necessary once you see and receive what you now hope for. True faith in God's eyes is hanging in there and trusting Him in spite of all you face, for you know His Word is true. That faith pleases God.

The climax of the first part of the book of Nehemiah is not verse 15 where you will read that the wall is finished. The lesson of faith and God's work through faith is that these men and women were willing to stand with Him and for Him through all that they faced to get it done. They had wielded, as

Paul would write to the Ephesians, the shield of faith by which they were able to quench all the fiery darts of the wicked one (Ephesians 6:16). Sometimes faith produces results slowly, but they are works worth waiting for. Noah labored building the ark with his sons for over 100 years without ever seeing a cloud in the sky or sprinkle to assure them rain would indeed come. Abraham wandered his entire life through a land that God said he could have; yet he didn't own any of it except a place to bury his body. Jeremiah spent over 50 years preaching and the only reaction was that people continually refused him, sought to silence him, and even tried to kill him. It is pleasing faith to wait patiently upon God to work, and it's in that process that we grow. James said the testing of your faith will produce patience (James 1:3). Nehemiah had been at this labor from its prayerful beginning and had faced some tough resistance. Now he is nearing the end, but Satan is not finished resisting him yet.

> *Now it happened when Sanballat, Tobiah, Geshem the Arab, and the rest of our enemies heard that I had rebuilt the wall, and that there were no breaks left in it (though at that time I had not hung the doors in the gates), that Sanballat and Geshem sent to me, saying, "Come, let us meet together among the villages in the plain of Ono." But they thought to do me harm.*
>
> *–Nehemiah 6:1-2*

This was the last-ditch attack on the heels of a ribbon-cutting ceremony. The wall was up and all that remained was to hang the doors. Here at the last moment, the enemy shows up singing a new song, "Can't we just be friends? Let's have lunch and let bygones be bygones." Note in our text that Nehemiah was aware of their deceit, "they thought to do me harm," he writes. One thing for sure, the enemy never rests, never cries uncle, and will try all methods to take you down. We find folks living with the great blessings of God upon their lives and then one day, all of a sudden, the wrath of the enemy to oppose and destroy seems to appear from nowhere. David fell with Bathsheba at a time when he had never lost a battle in his life. Jesus begins His public ministry at His baptism with a voice from heaven declaring of Him, "This is My beloved Son," and He is driven immediately into the wilderness and tested by the devil for 40 days and nights. He is later glorified on the Mount of Transfiguration, revealing Himself to three of His closest disciples, while down at the bottom of the hill, the rest of His disciples are frustrated because they were powerless to deliver a demon-possessed boy. It does seem that every mountaintop experience has a valley below waiting to challenge us yet again.

Now as the work is almost finished and its completion is already being planned, the enemy resurfaces, but this time with a completely different tactic. "Can we just get together and sort out our differences over lunch?" With the plains of Ono only 25 miles northwest of Jerusalem, Sanballat and Geshem's request sounded harmless enough. Nehemiah didn't see it that way at all. He had his spiritual antenna fully extended. He realized these men hadn't repented of their wickedness and still hated God and His people. Nothing had changed and there would be trouble waiting.

The Lord had spoken to Nehemiah's heart. He knew these guys were out to get him. And I think he had another tip: they wanted to meet in a place called Ono. If anyone ever invites you to "Oh no," don't go!

> *So I sent messengers to them, saying, "I am doing a great work, so that I cannot come down. Why should the work cease while I leave it and go down to you?" But they sent me this message four times, and I answered them in the same manner.*
>
> *–Nehemiah 6:3-4*

I don't know how Nehemiah's reply would have been

handled in those days, but if it were today, I'm sure the Jerusalem Post would have carried a headline that read "Governor Snubs Invitation To Peace Conference." I think one of the enemy's favorite tactics is to get us involved with seemingly innocent pursuits that sidetrack our relationship with, and service to, God. In and of themselves, these things might not be a problem, but to the degree that they replace or remove us from what God wants to do, they become a stumbling block. It's all about our priorities, isn't it?

"I can't stop the work," responds Nehemiah. Right priorities will inevitably protect you from the deceptions of the enemy. This city had been sitting without a wall for four generations. In all that time, why didn't someone look around and say, "We can't put up with this. Let's fix it?" I suspect it's the same reason we don't make the changes in our own walk with God we know we should. Insignificant activities and pursuits have a way of making their way to the top of the list, crowding out that which God would want to do. How many years have you vowed to make certain changes to your walk with God? What has kept you from doing it? I suspect it is the setting of priorities. You mean well, but the reason often is that something else has found its way to the top of your to-do list, crowding out what God would want you to do. One thing is sure: the enemy does not relent.

The apostle Paul, in writing to the Hebrews, was speaking to them about running the race to win and said in Hebrews 12:1, "Let us lay aside every weight, and the sin which so easily ensnares us, and let us run with endurance the race that is set before us." We know that sin will slow down and hamper our walks, but notice he also mentions "the weights." These are distinct from sin, but are nevertheless things that weigh on us and keep us from our full running potential. So here the invitation is from wicked men to mend fences when in reality they wanted to knock one wall down!

Notice that the enemy sent the same letter four times. "Come on down. How about lunch? How about dinner? How about breakfast? Brunch?" But I love Nehemiah's example because he just says, "I'm involved in the most important thing in my life and I can't let anything else get in the way." He had suspicions that these guys were up to no good and he was right as the next few verses bear out. Oh, that God would help us cry the same when the world offers us distractions, interruptions, and weights to slow us down from running for Him. In verse 13, Nehemiah will tell us that he saw it as a sin to stop doing what God had given him to do; to go out and do something else; to replace the vital with something far less important as, in this case, a deceptive invite from the enemy.

> *Then Sanballat sent his servant to me as before, the fifth time, with an open letter in his hand. In it was written: It is reported among the nations, and Geshem says, that you and the Jews plan to rebel; therefore, according to these rumors, you are rebuilding the wall, that you may be their king. And you have also appointed prophets to proclaim concerning you at Jerusalem, saying, "There is a king in Judah!" Now these matters will be reported to the king. So come, therefore, and let us consult together.*
>
> *–Nehemiah 6:5-7*

We might coin a new truism here: If at first you don't succeed, show your true colors. Notice that the fifth letter was a public letter. It was not written to be read by Nehemiah; it was written to be heard by others. The enemies' kindness was wearing thin; their true heart was exposed. They slandered Nehemiah, saying: "We plan to expose you and your evil motives of rebellion to the king. We know what you're up to. You're planning to take over. Once the wall is built, you'll ensconce yourself inside. There will be no getting you out. You've got false prophets proclaiming you're to be the king, according to your God. We hate to turn in these reports so we're giving you an opportunity to clear yourself. Just come and have some lunch. I'm sure we can put this ugly mess behind us and clear up any misunderstandings."

What's going on here? These are outright lies from the factory of hell! If Satan can't get you one way, he'll try some other way. And I would say to you, be careful when you become a tool in the enemy's hands by gossiping and lying about others, because notice here, this is a tool of the devil. Paul counseled the Ephesian saints, "Let no corrupt word proceed out of your mouth, but what is good for necessary edification, that it may impart grace to the hearers" (Ephesians 4:29). It is one of those defensive verses in the Bible that will protect you from the wiles of the enemy who seeks to use you to sow discord, bring complaint, undermine love, etc. But when the enemy speaks, he speaks according to the father of lies (John 8:44).

Notice in verse 6 that most rumors and lies don't have a source. One man, Geshem, was repeating what he had heard, but he supposedly heard it from unnamed sources: "they said," or "I've heard them say." Who are "they?" That's the way most rumors and innuendos begin. However, it can be effective, because if you discredit a leader, even by outright lies, you can sometimes bring him down. Courtroom lawyers know about this. Even though they know they will be reprimanded and challenged for a statement, claim, or leading question, they say what they want the jury to hear. When the objection is sustained, they willingly withdraw the question. But the words have been spoken by then, the impression made, and the innuendo remains.

Nehemiah is now placed publicly in a very difficult spot. He knows this letter is designed for only one purpose: to stop the work from being completed. But how could he let outright lies go unchallenged? Put yourself in his shoes. What would you do in his situation? Would you say, "Hey, wait a minute. That's a lie!"? Would you go and try to defend yourself? Would you take the risk of people believing them? Would you worry about whether it was going to get back to the king?

As a Christian, how do you handle criticism when it comes your way? It will come your way sometime for the world does not readily receive what you have to say, even if you say it kindly and mercifully. Here's what Nehemiah does:

> *Then I sent to him, saying, "No such things as you say are being done, but you invent them in your own heart." For they all were trying to make us afraid, saying, "Their hands will be weakened in the work, and it will not be done." Now therefore, O God, strengthen my hands.*
>
> *–Nehemiah 6:8-9*

Nehemiah's response to Sanballat was a firm public denial of the accusations. Yet, to the Lord privately in prayer, he admitted that the false charges made him nervous. Remember that the next time you expect too much of yourself. "What if the king buys this?" he wonders. "What if he comes and tears down the wall? What if he fires me or imprisons me or even worse?"

I like this picture because sometimes I think our faith can overwhelm our physical body's ability to stay calm. You believe God, but your hands are sweating. You're crying out for God, but your heart is racing. You know God's going to come through, but you can't get to sleep. It is the ultimate flesh versus spirit war within. David said, "For I hear the slander of many; Fear is on every side; While they take counsel together against me, They scheme to take away my life. But as for me, I trust in You, O LORD; I say, 'You are my God'" (Psalm 31:13-14). He knew the enemy. He knew what was going on. He knew what he potentially could face, but he went forward resting in his God.

Nehemiah says the same thing. He denied the accusations and then went back to work, back to serving the Lord. What would you have done? Most people, when slandered, retaliate. Most people run to their own defense. Most people will not sit idly by while folks speak evil of them. They will seek to clear the air. They will want to set the record straight. They will want to make sure everyone understands. This is not so for Nehemiah. He said, "That's a lie – and I've got work to do."

Look at Jesus. He was called a winebibber and a glutton, a friend of sinners, born out of wedlock, and a man of questionable motives. Yet we read of Him in 1 Peter 2:21, "For to this you were called, because Christ also suffered for us, leaving us an example, that you should follow His steps." Jesus was slandered much more and yet, committing Himself to the work of the Father, He pressed on.

Paul said in 1 Corinthians 4 that when the Lord comes, He's going to judge righteously and every man will have his portion from the Lord. Nehemiah was smart enough to let God protect the work and his integrity. He would not be sidelined or distracted, the work was great, and he would continue in it. The enemy here is defeated, but he is hardly ready to give up. He is always looking for another way to oppose God's work in you.

> *Afterward I came to the house of Shemaiah the son of Delaiah, the son of Mehetabel, who was a secret informer; and he said, "Let us meet together in the house of God, within the temple, and let us close the doors of the temple, for they are coming to kill you; indeed, at night they will come to kill you."*
>
> *–Nehemiah 6:10*

So here we go from pretense of friendship to threat of slander to now sending a wolf in sheep's clothing to say, "God has sent me to instruct you to run and hide." Satan is far more dangerous as an angel of light than he ever is as a roaring lion. Most of us know we have to get away from a roaring lion. But as an angel of light, he can work his way in. What did he say? We've got to run. We've got to hide. We've got to lock the doors. They're coming to kill you. You've got to get away. Satan will even work through feigned inspiration and religious phoniness. Being warned of his methods here, I look to see what our man Nehemiah will do or say. I like his response.

> *And I said, "Should such a man as I flee? And who is there such as I who would go into the temple to save his life? I will not go in!" Then I perceived that God had not sent him at all, but that he pronounced this prophecy against me because Tobiah and Sanballat had hired him. For this reason he was hired, that I should be afraid and act that way and sin, so that they might have cause for an evil report, that they might reproach me. My God, remember Tobiah and Sanballat, according to these their works, and the prophetess Noadiah and the rest of the prophets who would have made me afraid.*
>
> *–Nehemiah 6:11-14*

Nehemiah's response was awesome. He knew well the Lord he was serving and he was sure that what he was hearing was not something God would say. He also knew he was in a position where many people watched him and were influenced by his behavior and responses. "People look up to me," he said to himself. "I've been telling them how faithful God is. I can't be fearful now."

Fear is a great motivator to foolishness and sin, isn't it? Abraham takes Sarah to Egypt as they are running from a famine. He says to her, "You're far too beautiful. If you say you're my wife they're going to kill me and take you. So I have a plan. Say you're my sister." As far as I understand it, that still means they're going to take her; it's just that he's going to live. It wasn't a great plan for Sarah! Eventually Abraham's duplicity was rebuked by, of all people, an unbelieving Pharaoh (Genesis 12).

David goes to Achish where he shouldn't have been

and goes to hide with Goliath's sword in hand in Goliath's hometown. Not too bright but fear will make you do some foolish things. Found out by the king, David then acts as if he has lost his mind and is let go (1 Samuel 21).

Nehemiah's words here are great. "I'm not going to run. I'm not going to hide. I'm not going to save my life. I'm going to serve the Lord. If I run, that's sin. It will be sin for me, for the people – but even if it means my life, I'm staying put." Nehemiah didn't take vengeance. He just had to work through all of the plots of the enemy one by one in prayer and with the discernment of the Holy Spirit.

> *So the wall was finished on the twenty-fifth day of Elul, in fifty-two days. And it happened, when all our enemies heard of it, and all the nations around us saw these things, that they were very disheartened in their own eyes; for they perceived that this work was done by our God.*
>
> *–Nehemiah 6:15-16*

I love the fact that through it all God sustained His people, used the leadership of His servant, and, in the end, forced the enemies to see and acknowledge His work. To build a wall of this size in a little more than seven weeks would have been humanly impossible given the technology of Nehemiah's day. And yet after being in rubble heaps for 160 years, the wall now stood. Even the enemy had to admit that God was in it.

In Psalm 23:5-6, David worshiped the Lord with the words, "You prepare a table before me in the presence of my enemies; You anoint my head with oil; My cup runs over. Surely goodness and mercy shall follow me All the days of my life; And I will dwell in the house of the LORD Forever." Literally, "You feed me, nourish me, and care for me while my enemy stands by and watches." I appreciate that picture because although it doesn't always happen immediately, persistence in faith will bring us the kind of victory where even the enemy is going to have to admit that God is great.

Paul wrote to the Philippians, "But I want you to know, brethren, that the things which happened to me have actually turned out for the furtherance of the gospel" (Philippians 1:12). To the Corinthians, he said, "Therefore, my beloved brethren, be steadfast, immovable, always abounding in the work of the Lord, knowing that your labor is not in vain in the Lord" (1 Corinthians 15:58). God doesn't call us to initiate programs He can bless. He just asks us to be faithful vessels He can use and then He will work, even giving us victory over every plot and scheme of the enemy.

"Those who sow in tears Shall reap in joy," the psalmist declared in Psalm 126:5. Sometimes ministry is difficult. You plant in opposition, at great personal cost, without seeing much of a crop come forth. Then you wonder if it's really worth it, especially when the enemy seems more recognizable than the fruit of your labors. But look at the enemy's realized defeat here in verse 16. We can't stop the Lord's work, can we? We need to stick with it if we are going to see His best and see the enemy overthrown.

You can't stop reading the Bible. You can't stop going to church. You can't stop serving people. You can't stop sharing the Lord. Life is hard, sure, but the enemy is going to have to one day look at the life you lived and say, "God did that."

> *Also in those days the nobles of Judah sent many letters to Tobiah, and the letters of Tobiah came to them. For many in Judah were pledged to him, because he was the son-in-law of Shechaniah the son of Arah, and his son Jehohanan had married the daughter of Meshullam the son of Berechiah. Also they reported his good deeds before me, and reported my words to him. Tobiah sent letters to frighten me.*
>
> *–Nehemiah 6:17-19*

These last few verses in chapter 6 introduce us to the

new and present danger for Nehemiah and the Jews in Jerusalem. The wall is up and the people are safe, but the enemy is hardly finished. Now he moves some of his agents inside the walls among the people. Tobiah had a lot of supporters among the Jews in large part due to the fact that both he and his son had married Jewish women. The enemy was now in the camp by a secret alliance that was deeper than friendship; it was family. However, it wasn't spiritual. It sets the scene for us as we move to the last portion of the book.

We have to learn from Nehemiah that there's an absolute necessity for you and I to push through the storms and the trials by faith, keeping our eyes on the Lord and His Word, and relying on His power and might. Whatever is in the way, we're going to have victory in Jesus. As you read the whole Bible. you'll find that you can have peace that passes all understanding. You can have joy unspeakable and be full of glory. Let's see what the next chapters have in store for us as we seek the Lord through His Word.

Part Two

Revival

Chapter 9

Steps To Personal Revival (Part 1)

Nehemiah 7

In chapter 6, the wall was finished. But that was only half of the story because, though the people were more secure physically, they still had little security in their own personal relationship with God. Beginning here in chapter 7, the focus shifts from the construction of the wall to the reconstruction of the spiritual lives of the people. In many ways, the focus also shifts from Nehemiah, the governor and overseer, to Ezra, the scribe whom we are introduced to in Ezra 2 as a man who feared the Lord, was well-versed in Scripture, and was skillful in the Law of Moses.

The city itself had fallen to Babylon in 606-605 BC. Seventy years later, in 536 BC, when they were allowed to return, nearly 50,000 folks did head out of the metropolis of Babylon for the Jerusalem that lie in ruins, where God had put His name. Then 79 years later, Ezra came there with 2,000 servants – mostly worship leaders and priests who would serve in the temple. Another 13 years passed before Nehemiah came. From the time Jerusalem was first invaded until where we are here, 161 years had gone by and four generations had passed. Most of the folks who now lived in Jerusalem were ignorant, not only of the history of God's dealing with Jerusalem, but they lacked any sense or understanding of God's Word. They had either been raised in captivity or had come here with family now dead and buried. They needed to come to know their God and the promises of God found in His Word.

The city of Jerusalem now possessed a wall and a temple, but there was a tremendous spiritual vacuum among the people. History tells us that in captivity most of the Jews lost their ability to read and write Hebrew, adopting rather the Aramaic or Chaldean language of their captors. It left them without personal access to God's Word, which over the next 450 years would be taught to them by the scribes and later the Pharisees, who studied Hebrew and the Scriptures, but re-interpreted the Bible as they saw fit. In the process, the people of God were being steered away from obedience and grace to a religious system of their own design, religious ways never found in God's Word, ways that were devoid of His grace and mercy. I hope that will convince you that there's no substitute for knowing the Bible yourself, that knowing God's Word is the best safeguard against being led astray. Unfortunately today there are many churches that do not teach the Bible on a regular basis from cover to cover. That was the position the people with Nehemiah now found themselves in. They had a beautiful new wall and they were secure once again. Now Nehemiah's interest turns to their spiritual well-being.

> *Then it was, when the wall was built and I had hung the doors, when the gatekeepers, the singers, and the Levites had been appointed, that I gave the charge of Jerusalem to my brother Hanani, and Hananiah the leader of the citadel, for he was a faithful man and feared God more than many. And I said to them, "Do not let the gates of Jerusalem be opened until the sun is hot; and while they stand guard, let them shut and bar the doors; and appoint guards from among the inhabitants of Jerusalem, one at his watch station and another in front of his own house." Now the city was large and spacious, but the people in it were few, and the houses were not rebuilt.*
>
> *–Nehemiah 7:1-4*

Nehemiah's last official task was to provide security. The qualifications in verse 2 were much like those Paul uses for deacons in 1 Timothy 3, faithfulness based upon the fear of the Lord. Gatekeepers and neighborhood watches were in place. The city was as secure as it could be; but what the people needed more than security was spiritual life.

> *Then my God put it into my heart to gather the nobles, the rulers, and the people, that they might be registered by genealogy. And I found a register of the genealogy of those who had come up in the first return, and found written in it: These are the people of the province who came back from the captivity, of those who had been carried away, whom Nebuchadnezzar the king of Babylon had carried away, and who returned to Jerusalem and Judah, everyone to his city.*
>
> *–Nehemiah 7:5-6*

From here through verse 77, we are given a list of descendants that had been kept or found. The Old Testament had specific laws regarding who could serve in the temple and the priesthood based on the lines of Levi and Aaron. So we read here some of the recorded genealogical accounts of their lineage to ensure the Old Testament law would be followed in choosing those who would serve in the spiritual activities of the nation. If they were going to start worshiping the Lord as a people regularly once again, they wanted to be sure they were doing it in the way God had specifically prescribed. Revival always starts with God's people returning to seek to do things God's way and so it was here.

From verses 64-65, we learn some that were willing to serve were not able to verify their lineage and so they weren't allowed at that time to serve as priests. So some were set aside and everyone agreed with this action as they longed to go back to worshiping together at the temple.

In verses 66-67, we are told that the entire number of

people who came in that first repatriation was 49,942. Ezra brought an additional 2,000 families or so 79 years later.

Chapter 10

Steps To Personal Revival (Part 2)

Nehemiah 8

In chapter 8, we find the first recorded spiritual revival since the people returned from captivity almost 100 years earlier. It should interest you that every revival in the Bible and throughout history begins not among unbelievers, but among believers. In these revivals, we see a work of God beginning again, among people who already knew the Lord – oftentimes for a great deal of time – who again have interest in, and hunger for, the Word of God and to applying it to their daily lives.

Here the people, both individually and collectively, began to experience this desire in their hearts to return to the Lord and His ways. I suspect hearing and seeing all God had done in the building of the wall encouraged them to seek Him all the more. Revival had come to Jerusalem and they focused upon God's Word and the authority that it was to hold in their lives.

> *Now all the people gathered together as one man in the open square that was in front of the Water Gate; and they told Ezra the scribe to bring the Book of the Law of Moses, which the LORD had commanded Israel.*
>
> *–Nehemiah 8:1*

This is the first time in centuries God's people had been able to gather together publicly without fear. Nehemiah brought Ezra to read the Word of God to them. It reminds me of Barnabas in Acts 11 when he arrived in Antioch. God began to use him mightily. Daily salvations were commonplace. As the church began to grow, Barnabas realized teaching was not his gift and so he set out to find Paul. When he did, he brought him to Antioch and he became the pastor of this church that would become the center for world missions in the first century, instrumental in spreading the gospel around the world.

Here with Nehemiah, tens of thousands of people were gathered in the open square together to hear the Word of God for themselves, which was quite a change from three chapters earlier when we had seen them all terrified and wanting to quit the work. Revival had begun and it had come through the Word of God! It is the prayer of every pastor for the church that God might revive His people. It is always my prayer as well. You don't want to grow cold or lukewarm, indifferent or settled in. You want to have that hunger for the Lord that you had the first day you met Him, where you stood in line to get into Bible study, where you came early to get a seat, where the people gathered because God's Word was being taught, and there was a hunger to know what He wanted to say to you.

> *So Ezra the priest brought the Law before the assembly of men and women and all who could hear with understanding on the first day of the seventh month. Then he read from it in the open square that was in front of the Water Gate from morning until midday, before the men and women and those who could understand; and the ears of all the people were attentive to the Book of the Law.*
>
> *–Nehemiah 8:2-3*

The first day of the seventh month is an important day in the Jewish calendar. It is the Jewish New Year, Rosh Hashanah, the Feast of Trumpets. We are told here that Ezra read from morning until midday, which means he read for about six hours. Interestingly enough, the people were attentive to what he had to say for all that time. Ezra didn't keep peoples' attention with stories of courage or adventure that would appeal to their imaginations. He didn't keep them there with his strong personality or promises of prizes for those who would endure. They were there simply standing, hearing, and receiving because they were hungry to hear what God had to say. Some of them hadn't heard it taught for years. Some of them had never heard God's Word taught at all.

In Jeremiah 29:13, the prophet declared, "And you will seek Me and find Me, when you search for Me with all your heart." In other words, it's going to require that kind of dedicated hunger to really find God and His best for your life. And you read here that all of the people gathered and they attentively listened with understanding to the reading of God's Word.

> *So Ezra the scribe stood on a platform of wood which they had made for the purpose; and beside him, at his right hand, stood Mattithiah, Shema, Anaiah, Urijah, Hilkiah, and Maaseiah; and at his left hand Pedaiah, Mishael, Malchijah, Hashum, Hashbadana, Zechariah, and Meshullam. And Ezra opened the book in the sight of all the people, for he was standing above all the people; and when he opened it, all the people stood up.*
>
> *–Nehemiah 8:4-5*

On a wooden pulpit raised above the people, along with 13 others who would help him, Ezra began to read God's Word. For the next several verses down to verse 18, God in this narrative gives us some important insights into how we can be personally revived.

We read in verse 5 that as the Word was opened, the people stood up. The first step in any revival is a reverence for the Word of God. Ezra opened the book and everyone came to their feet. They weren't sitting back half-asleep, looking at their sundials, griping about how long Ezra was going. No, they stood as he read for six hours, because they were so hungry to hear. More vital to revival than anything else is a hunger to hear what God has to say. How hungry are you? There's a good way for you to determine how hungry you are in your heart for the Word of God. Ask yourself how disappointed you are when a Bible study is over? Do you wish it had gone longer? Or are you glad it is finally over?

It used to be in Jesus' day that the teacher would sit and the people would stand. How that got turned around, I do not know! Additionally, consider that in the days of Nehemiah, even as it would be in the first century, to have a copy of the Scriptures for yourself was unheard of. Today we have such unprecedented access to His Word. We have 17 versions or more on our shelves or on our computer. But these people had almost no direct access to the Scriptures. Even in the Middle Ages before the printing press, Bibles were chained to the pillars of the churches in England and people would stand in line for hours just to get a chance to read it for themselves.

Here when the people were given access to the Scriptures, they came with tremendous excitement and hunger that led to revival. We struggle to read through the entire Bible in a year and then wonder why we aren't seeing a revival. The first necessary step to any revival is what you find here among the people, a hunger to hear from God.

> *And Ezra blessed the LORD, the great God. Then all the people answered, "Amen, Amen!" while lifting up their hands. And they bowed their heads and worshiped the LORD with their faces to the ground.*
>
> *–Nehemiah 8:6*

If reverence for the Word is first, a desire to worship God has to follow. In any revival, there is a refocusing of our interest on the things of God. Here, as Ezra began to praise the Lord, the people joined in. They raised their hands, they bowed their heads, they humbled themselves.

> *Also Jeshua, Bani, Sherebiah, Jamin, Akkub, Shabbethai, Hodijah, Maaseiah, Kelita, Azariah, Jozabad, Hanan, Pelaiah, and the Levites, helped the people to understand the Law; and the people stood in their place. So they read distinctly from the book, in the Law of God; and they gave the sense, and helped them to understand the reading.*
>
> –*Nehemiah 8:7-8*

In addition to reverence for the Scriptures and a worshipful heart, the third element of revival is expositional teaching, where people are helped to understand what God has said. Note the words here in our text: "read distinctly," as they gave sense and understanding to the reading, helping the people to understand the Word of God. The real key to growth and revival is to read God's Word and understand it in the setting or context in which it is given. It is the desperate need of the church today.

We have available in our church bookstore a recorded Bible study on every verse in the Bible. I think every church should commit themselves to that so their people would know God's Word. Unfortunately, that's not always the case. Some churches have never even ventured into the Old Testament. Others stay away from Revelation or the books of the prophets.

I think one of the greatest contributions of the Calvary Chapel movement over the years has been its dependence upon teaching God's Word and its willingness to let God's Word be the final word for all we need. You can have a "Fill A Pew Night," or a "Revival Week," or a "Church Month," or "40 Days of Purpose," but what are you going to do on day 41 and day 57 and 3 months from Tuesday when you go to the doctor and hear you might have terminal cancer? People need to know God's Word and they need to have it taught to them. It can't be some unstable, temporary, interest based on some multi-media show that arouses an emotional response.

"My people are destroyed for lack of knowledge," God declared through His prophet, Hosea (Hosea 4:6a). Job would say to the Lord, "I have not departed from the commandments of His lip; I have treasured the words of His mouth More than my necessary food" (Job 23:12).

We need to have the Word of God taught to us. Speaking through Isaiah, the Lord said, "For as the rain comes down, and the snow from heaven, And do not return there, But water the earth, And make it bring forth and bud, That it may give seed to the sower And bread to the eater, So shall My word be that goes forth from My mouth; It shall not return to Me void, But it shall accomplish what I please, And it shall prosper in the thing for which I sent it" (Isaiah 55:10-11).

Karl Armeding, one of the presidents of Moody Bible Institute, once said, "I'm not a very good preacher. I just want to explain the Bible." In my opinion, that is really the best preacher of all.

> *And Nehemiah, who was the governor, Ezra the priest and scribe, and the Levites who taught the people said to all the people, "This day is holy to the LORD your God; do not mourn nor weep." For all the people wept, when they heard the words of the Law.*
>
> *–Nehemiah 8:9*

The fourth element of any revival is the personal application of the Scriptures to our lives. This isn't as obvious as it might sound because you can certainly attend church regularly while keeping your distance from the truth of God. You can listen for information: "Well, that's very interesting. I never thought about it like that ..." Or you can analyze the presentation: "He didn't look in my direction very much." You can listen for application to someone else: "You know who should have been here today? Uncle Fred. He really needs to hear this." In all of those responses you are able to push the Scriptures away from you. They don't have to apply to you. They apply to anyone but you, because the danger of applying it to you is that you might have to do something about it. Often folks will choose churches that preach messages that do not convict or demand change. Yet we read in God's Word, "For the word of God is living and powerful, and sharper than any two-edged sword, piercing even to the division of soul and spirit, and of joints and marrow, and is a discerner of the thoughts and intents of the heart. And there is no creature hidden from His sight, but all things are naked and open to the eyes of Him to whom we must give account" (Hebrews 4:12-13). God desires to perform spiritual surgery on each of us personally!

Here in Nehemiah, as the people listened, they didn't listen for someone else; they listened for themselves. Though it was a joyful season, a festival of rejoicing in God's blessing, the people could do nothing but weep over how much they realized they had failed God, how little they had done to please Him, and how far they had moved away from Him. Hearing of the desires of God and His great love, while realizing the wasted years in their past and the sinfulness of their lives, moved them to tears.

When Paul wrote to the Corinthians he told them, "For even if I made you sorry with my letter, I do not regret it; though I did regret it. For I perceive that the same epistle made you sorry, though only for a while. Now I rejoice, not that you were made sorry, but that your sorrow led to repentance. For you were made sorry in a godly manner, that you might suffer loss from us in nothing" (2 Corinthians 7:8-9). Revival begins when you come to church to hear what God wants to say to you!

> *Then he said to them, "Go your way, eat the fat, drink the sweet, and send portions to those for whom nothing is prepared; for this day is holy to our Lord. Do not sorrow, for the joy of the LORD is your strength." So the Levites quieted all the people, saying, "Be still, for the day is holy; do not be grieved." And all the people*

went their way to eat and drink, to send portions and rejoice greatly, because they understood the words that were declared to them.

–Nehemiah 8:10-12

Faith will lead to repentance and repentance will bring joy, which is always God's plan for you. The joy of the Lord can be your strength. Peter said, "Whom having not seen you love. Though now you do not see Him, yet believing, you rejoice with joy inexpressible and full of glory" (1 Peter 1:8). Jesus said, "These things I have spoken to you, that My joy may remain in you, and that your joy may be full" (John 15:11). So here the people were encouraged to go home and rejoice which they did because they understood what God had taught them: God's Word changes lives and brings joy.

Now on the second day the heads of the fathers' houses of all the people, with the priests and Levites, were gathered to Ezra the scribe, in order to understand the words of the Law. And they found written in the Law, which the LORD had commanded by Moses, that the children of Israel should dwell in booths during the feast of the seventh month, and that they should announce and proclaim in all their cities and in Jerusalem, saying, "Go out to the mountain, and bring olive branches, branches of oil trees, myrtle branches, palm branches, and branches of leafy trees, to make booths, as it is written." Then the people went out and brought them and made themselves booths, each one on the roof of his house, or in their courtyards or the courts of the house of God, and in the open square of the Water Gate and in the open square of the Gate of Ephraim. So the whole assembly of those who had returned from the captivity made booths and sat under the booths; for since the days of Joshua the son of Nun until that day the children of Israel had not done so. And there was very great gladness. Also day by day, from the first day until the last day, he read from the Book of the Law of God. And they kept the feast seven days; and on the eighth day there was a sacred assembly, according to the prescribed manner.

–Nehemiah 8:13-18

Here's one last step when it comes to personal revival: You must have a willingness of heart to simply obey what God has to say. Notice that on the second day of the feast, the leadership folks got together to try and make some policies for the nation based upon the Scriptures. One of the things they discovered was that there was to be a Feast of Succoth, Tabernacles, or Booths. Beginning on the fifteenth day of the seventh month and lasting for a week, the folks were to build little booths, or lean-tos, to live in for a week as reminders of how God had provided for their ancestors for 40 years in the wilderness. Although the nation hadn't celebrated this feast for nearly 800 years, these revived hearts were committed to doing what God said. Simple obedience is clearly the way that God blesses; by daily, small steps of obedience.

I suspect the enemy that opposed the wall would have opposed this as well. I can hear Tobiah saying, "First it was that lousy wall. Now it's these disgusting booths." If you remember your school days when you were assigned some building project that would then be seen by all, there always seemed to be one overachiever who made his look perfect and no one appreciated it but him. He was the one with the four story building made entirely out of popsicle sticks while yours looked like someone had sat on a box of popsicle sticks. There are no instructions anywhere in the Bible for how to build these booths so I'm sure some came with a patio and a swing while others had a condemned sign. But it didn't matter. God wasn't interested in how the thing looked. He was just interested in obedience.

We read in verse 17 that the result of their willing obedience was "very great gladness." That is quite a description. Not gladness or even great gladness, but very great gladness! I know some believers who always seem miserable and, because obedience brings joy, I suspect it might be simply because they aren't really seeking to do what God has said.

In review, the six steps that lead to revival are (1) reverence for the Word, (2) a worshipful heart, (3) exposing ourselves to the teaching of the Word that fills us with understanding, (4) applying the Word of God personally, (5) letting faith lead from repentance to joy, and (6) doing what we have heard. Maybe you've known the Lord for quite some time now but you've grown cold. Review your own life in light of these six principles and let the Lord bring His fire to your heart again.

Chapter 11

A Nation Returns Home

Nehemiah 9

Now on the twenty-fourth day of this month the children of Israel were assembled with fasting, in sackcloth, and with dust on their heads. Then those of Israelite lineage separated themselves from all foreigners; and they stood and confessed their sins and the iniquities of their fathers. And they stood up in their place and read from the Book of the Law of the LORD their God for one-fourth of the day; and for another fourth they confessed and worshiped the LORD their God. Then Jeshua, Bani, Kadmiel, Shebaniah, Bunni, Sherebiah, Bani, and Chenani stood on the stairs of the Levites and cried out with a loud voice to the LORD their God.
–Nehemiah 9:1-4

I love this chapter because it shows me the influence of God's Word on receptive hearts. We find here one of the longest single recorded prayers in the Bible. It was offered to the Lord from a people who had been spending a great deal of time in His Word. This prayer reflected what had taken place in their hearts as His Word had washed over them day after day. This people, with great heritage and a great history, had set God aside for generations, but had now returned to the God who loved them so.

Like most prayers in the Scriptures recorded for us, there are key elements that we always find. One is a looking back to God's faithfulness in times past. We were told (8:3) that the gathered people stood for six hours as God's Word was read to them loudly and the leaders gave sense to it (8:8). I don't suspect that six hours was typical, but when there's a hungry heart that can't get enough, even that may seem too short. His Word affected them deeply. God spoke clearly through it to their hearts. No one needed to encourage them to be hungry; they were hungry.

The Feast of Tabernacles took place from the 15th-22nd of the seventh month. Here, it is the 24th, just a day later, and the people are gathered again; not by religious mandate, but by their own desire to continue to draw near to God. They arrive wearing sackcloth with dust on their heads, which were outward signs of sorrow and repentance. Though God had begun this work nationally, they now each individually resolved to seek Him.

Jerusalem was still in dire straits. The people had a wall around the city but the enemy surrounded them and they were impoverished. Only a few people actually lived in town behind those new walls. In spite of that, the last couple of months, under the leadership of Nehemiah and the teaching of God's Word by Ezra, had brought revival!

The prescribed religious calendar had come and gone, and yet they were still hungry for more of Him. In modern terms, you could say, they were in church and it wasn't even Christmas, or Easter, or even Sunday! They had gathered on an "off-day," just because they wanted more of the Lord in their lives. And notice that they were doing the very things God, in His Word, had demanded of them: to separate themselves from the world and to acknowledge God publicly. They looked to the Lord with anticipation of His answers and fellowship. I love the fact that God's Word in the hearts of the people brings them to a place where they just can't get enough of Him. So the people find themselves on an unscheduled day spontaneously coming by the thousands to mourn their sin and seek His face.

If I asked you what God has taught you from the Bible this past month that has changed your life, what would your answer be? Spiritual growth, after all, does not come from a routine, or a habit, or from some religious calendar. It comes from God speaking to your heart and you responding to Him in love and obedience. That's where we find these saints here in chapter 9. If you can't say what God has taught you the past month that has changed your life, I suspect that is because you have not exposed yourself enough to His Word. He's talking plenty; we just need to be listening more. That's what was happening here. They stood everyday and came to know their God, the God of the Bible, again.

> *And the Levites, Jeshua, Kadmiel, Bani, Hashabniah, Sherebiah, Hodijah, Shebaniah, and Pethahiah, said: "Stand up and bless the LORD your God Forever and ever! Blessed be Your glorious name, Which is exalted above all blessing and praise! You alone are the LORD; You have made heaven, The heaven of heavens, with all their host, The earth and everything on it, The seas and all that is in them, And You preserve them all. The host of heaven worships You.*
>
> *–Nehemiah 9:5-6*

I love the fact that this nation, that hadn't had a Bible study in 100 years, heard the Word and came away with the ability to properly identify God. Throughout Scripture, every prayer from the hearts of people hungry to know God is the result of a proper understanding of Him. These folks had it right, didn't they? They said of the Lord, "You're our Creator and our Preserver. You have made us. You can keep us. You're the God of gods. There is no one like You. Everything You have created, the host of heaven, worships You. Everything we see, You've made. Everything we see, You've kept."

> *"You are the LORD God, Who chose Abram, And brought him out of Ur of the Chaldeans, And gave him the name Abraham; You found his heart faithful before You, And made a covenant with him To give the land of the Canaanites, the Hittites, the Amorites, the Perizzites, the Jebusites, and the Girgashites — To give it to his descendants. You have performed Your words, For You are righteous."*
>
> *–Nehemiah 9:7-8*

"God, You chose us according to Your will," the people prayed. And they were right. God chose Abraham, then He chose Israel, then He chose you. We are a chosen generation, Peter tells us (1 Peter 2:9). I wouldn't have chosen me nor most of you. And, looking around the church, it's pretty clear God got the raw deal picking us. He gets us, we get Him. Guess who wins.

So the people are hearing from the Bible and here are the conclusions they draw: "God, You're faithful. You picked us. You promised things to us. You saw us as faithful and You blessed us. Promises made. Word kept. God is dependable." They were learning by leaps and bounds and growing like weeds.

> *"You saw the affliction of our fathers in Egypt, And heard their cry by the Red Sea. You showed signs and wonders against Pharaoh, Against all his servants, And against all the people of his land. For You knew that they acted proudly against them. So You made a name for Yourself, as it is this day. And You divided the sea before them, So that they went through the midst of the sea on the dry land; And their persecutors You threw into the deep, As a stone into the mighty waters. Moreover You led them by day with a cloudy pillar, And by night with a pillar of fire, To give them light on the road Which they should travel. You came down*

> *also on Mount Sinai, And spoke with them from heaven, And gave them just ordinances and true laws, Good statutes and commandments. You made known to them Your holy Sabbath, And commanded them precepts, statutes and laws, By the hand of Moses Your servant. You gave them bread from heaven for their hunger, And brought them water out of the rock for their thirst, And told them to go in to possess the land Which You had sworn to give them."*
>
> *–Nehemiah 9:9-15*

"You saw the affliction of our fathers in Egypt." They learned that God is always aware of our condition. That's an important truth to know. Many people today ask, "Well, if God cares for me, where is He? If God knows what I'm going through, what is He doing about it?" Yet you will not hear that from these revived lives. They read the archives of the history of God's dealing in the Bible and came to the conclusion that God saw where they were and had come to help them. They had it right. God is always near. God is always available. He had come to their rescue in Egypt. He had seen them through the Red Sea and delivered them through it. He knew what they needed even now. How awesome to know the Lord better each day by His Word.

> *"But ..."*
>
> *–Nehemiah 9:16a*

The people in Nehemiah's day were reading the Scriptures and concluding that God was faithful. The problem was that, although God was faithful, His people had not been, sometimes for long periods of time, which is what had brought this nation to pray this day with sackcloth, ashes, and fasting. God is good. God is faithful, but ...

> *"... they and our fathers acted proudly, Hardened their necks, And did not heed Your commandments. They refused to obey, And they were not mindful of Your wonders That You did among them. But they hardened their necks, And in their rebellion They appointed a leader To return to their bondage. But You are God, Ready to pardon, Gracious and merciful, Slow to anger, Abundant in kindness, And did not forsake them."*
>
> *–Nehemiah 9:16b-17*

I love how repentance brings revival and a changed outlook. The people realized God had been ever so faithful and they had not! The old saying is true: If there's ever distance between you and God, guess who moved. Yet many blame God for their situations. True repentance has the people admitting it was they who had turned from God, but notice God didn't turn from them.

That's a life-changing truth to learn - that God doesn't respond in kind. I've heard people say, "The God of the Old Testament is brutal." Not true. In Exodus 33:20-23, when Moses told God he wanted to see Him, it says, "But He said 'You cannot see My face; for no man shall see Me, and live.' And the LORD said, 'Here is a place by Me, and you shall stand on the rock. So it shall be, while My glory passes by that I will put you in the cleft of the rock, and cover you with My hand while I pass by. Then I will take away My hand, and you shall see My back; but My face shall not be seen.'" Moses settled for that and his conclusion was, "The LORD, the LORD God, merciful and gracious, longsuffering and abounding in goodness and truth" (Exodus 34:6). The God of the Old Testament is merciful. God doesn't change.

I can't for the life of me understand why God is so merciful to us. I don't know how long He would have been willing to put up with the life of prostitution Mary Magdalene had chosen or the murderous ways of a self-righteous Paul, or the thief on the cross who grabbed for whatever straw he could at the last minute, or that stinking prodigal son who came home because he had nothing left having spent it all on less than honorable endeavors. Yet God put up with all of them. If you were God, wouldn't you at some point say, "That's enough!"? But He didn't, not with these and not with us. His people were learning of His heart by reading His Word.

> *"Even when they made a molded calf for themselves, And said, 'This is your god That brought you up out of Egypt,' And worked great provocations, Yet in Your manifold mercies You did not forsake them in the wilderness. The pillar of the cloud did not depart from them by day, To lead them on the road; Nor the pillar of fire by night, To show them light, And the way they should go. You also gave Your good Spirit to instruct them, And did not withhold Your manna from their mouth And gave them water for their thirst."*
>
> *–Nehemiah 9:18-20*

How did God respond to the unfaithfulness of His people? He did so by blessing them, by being good to them, and by guiding and providing for them. He loved them still. Most people don't have this concept of God, but it's the biblical one. Is He a God of judgment? Of course. But He is first a God of redemption, of grace and mercy, and loving-kindness and long-suffering.

> *"Forty years You sustained them in the wilderness; They lacked nothing; Their clothes did not wear out And their feet did not swell."*
>
> *–Nehemiah 9:21*

Miracle after miracle after miracle was required to sustain an entire nation in the inhospitable wilderness for 40 years. Although the people depended on God's love every day for their sustenance and safety, they often refused Him openly when it came to obedience to His ways. That sounds much like many of us who want and depend upon His blessings but want little of Him beyond that. They continued to look back at their history with God and learn of His heart, even in times of great rebellion.

> *"Moreover You gave them kingdoms and nations, And divided them into districts. So they took possession of the land of Sihon, The land of the king of Heshbon, And the land of Og king of Bashan. You also multiplied their children as the stars of heaven, And brought them into the land Which You had told their fathers To go in and possess. So the people went in And possessed the land; You subdued before them the inhabitants of the land, The Canaanites, And gave them into their hands, With their kings And the people of the land, That they might do with them as they wished. And they took strong cities and a rich land, And possessed houses full of all goods, Cisterns already dug, vineyards, olive groves, And fruit trees in abundance. So they ate and were filled and grew fat, And delighted themselves in Your great goodness."*
>
> *–Nehemiah 9:22-25*

In other words, God gave to a rebellious people everything He promised. He blessed them in childbearing, He gave them earthly possessions, and they possessed the land He had promised to them. Psalm 44:3 tells us that they didn't gain possession of the land of Canaan by the sword nor did their own arm save them but it was God's right hand that provided all. It was God's arm. It was the light of His countenance. It was His grace.

When Moses sat the people down in Deuteronomy for some final instructions before they finally went into the land, he warned them in chapter 8:11, "Beware that you do not forget the LORD your God by not keeping His commandments,

His judgments, and His statutes which I command you today." But that's exactly what happened. Even in their wickedness, God had blessed them. Yet they forgot Him. They delighted themselves in God's goods, but they didn't want anything to do with His goodness. They lived in God's good land, but they didn't want God's good Law. They wanted God's blessing. They didn't want God.

The people gathering here and looking back realized that, which is why we find them weeping in sackcloth and ashes. The feast days had been joyful but the reality was they were brokenhearted as they recognized that they were in danger of letting history repeat itself again. "God help us," they prayed. "God help us," we pray as well.

> *"Nevertheless they were disobedient And rebelled against You, Cast Your law behind their backs And killed Your prophets, who testified against them To turn them to Yourself; And they worked great provocations. Therefore You delivered them into the hand of their enemies, Who oppressed them; And in the time of their trouble, When they cried to You, You heard from heaven; And according to Your abundant mercies You gave them deliverers who saved them From the hand of their enemies. But after they had rest, They again did evil before You. Therefore You left them in the hand of their enemies, So that they had dominion over them; Yet when they returned and cried out to You, You heard from heaven; And many times You delivered them according to Your mercies, And testified against them, That You might bring them back to Your law. Yet they acted proudly, And did not heed Your commandments, But sinned against Your judgments, 'Which if a man does, he shall live by them.' And they shrugged their shoulders, Stiffened their necks, And would not hear. Yet for many years You had patience with them, And testified against them by Your Spirit in Your prophets.*

> *Yet they would not listen; Therefore You gave them into the hand of the peoples of the lands. Nevertheless in Your great mercy You did not utterly consume them nor forsake them; For You are God, gracious and merciful."*
>
> *–Nehemiah 9:26-31*

The rebellion repeated itself time and again in the nation's history, but God continued to greatly love His people. He would send a captor to them, or someone who treated them harshly, who taxed them too much, or who made their lives extremely difficult. Nearly every time the people would eventually conclude, "We hate living like this. Oh, God, our God, help us. We're sorry." Each time God heard their cries and sent a deliverer. Relieved, the people would settle in for a time before falling right back into their sinful ways. Soon God would send another to overthrow them and the process would begin all over again. This cycle went on for over 300 years during the days of the judges.

Following the judges, God gave the people kings and yet they still rebelled. Eventually the nation split into two upon the death of Solomon. In the north, the nation called Israel would see 19 wicked kings from nine different families leading the nation astray for 209 years before the Assyrians overthrew them once and for all in 722 BC. In the south, the nation of Judah, comprised only of Judah and Benjamin, stayed in Jerusalem where God had placed His name. They would see 20 kings from the same family during this time of division, eight of them godly kings. They lasted for 325 years before they were carried away to Babylon for 70 years as God dealt with their idolatry and sin.

At some point, if I were God, I might have declared, "I'm taking my cloud and my pillar of fire and I'm going home. Good luck finding your way out of the desert." But here's the interesting thing: The people praying this prayer were the evidence that God had remained faithful because they were praying it in Jerusalem, in the Promised Land.

God continued to deal with His people for one purpose: that He might bring them to Himself. God wants fellowship. That's why He made you. He is patient, He is kind, and He extends His mercy to anyone who calls on His name. The nation here with Nehemiah was broken before Him and receiving His love and forgiveness.

> *"Now therefore, our God, The great, the mighty, and awesome God, Who keeps covenant and mercy: Do not let all the trouble seem small before You That has come upon us, Our kings and our princes, Our priests and our prophets, Our fathers and on all Your people, From the days of the kings of Assyria until this day. However You are just in all that has befallen us; For You have dealt faithfully, But we have done wickedly."*
>
> *–Nehemiah 9:32-33*

In two verses, you can recognize immediately what God has done in the lives of these folks. They had learned more about Him in two months than in the previous 100 years. Their conclusion was very clear: "God, we're in big trouble here. But it isn't Your fault. You have always been faithful, always reliable, always there for us." If you ever come to the point where you're praying and you somehow come up with the words, "God, if You're so fair … " or "God, if You're so good … " or "God, if You're so just …" then I would suggest you go back and read some more, because you don't see Him as He truly is. The people of God here saw clearly this day.

In Lamentations 3:39, Jeremiah asks, "Why should a living man complain, A man for the punishment of his sins?" And Ezra said to the Lord, "And after all that has come upon us for our evil deeds and for our great guilt, since You our God have punished us less than our iniquities deserve, and have given us such deliverance as this" (Ezra 9:13). That's the proper concept of God and you hear it here from the people. "God, please don't write us off because we're in grave trouble as a nation." And they were. "We've made our bed and this trouble is self-induced. But we are now on our knees, with dirt on our heads, because we want You back." That's their prayer.

> *"Neither our kings nor our princes, Our priests nor our fathers, Have kept Your law, Nor heeded Your commandments and Your testimonies, With which You testified against them. For they have not served You in their kingdom, Or in the many good things that You gave them, Or in the large and rich land which You set before them; Nor did they turn from their wicked works. Here we are, servants today! And the land that You gave to our fathers, To eat its fruit and its bounty, Here we are, servants in it! And it yields much increase to the kings You have set over us, Because of our sins; Also they have dominion over our bodies and our cattle At their pleasure; And we are in great distress. And because of all this, We make a sure covenant and write it; Our leaders, our Levites, and our priests seal it."*
>
> *–Nehemiah 9:34-38*

Proclaiming their guilt and God's goodness, the people's prayer request is simple: "We want to start over. We want to make a new covenant. We'll put it in writing. We'll testify to it publicly. We'll sign on the dotted line in the presence of our priests." Learning from their past, they seek to make their future better by committing their present to God. They were right. God will allow them to start over. He is the God of new beginnings. Isaiah declared, "Let the wicked forsake his way, And the unrighteous man his thoughts; Let him return to the LORD, And He will have mercy on him; And to our God, For He will abundantly pardon" (Isaiah 55:7).

The people were counting on God's pardon and they knew they could because there hadn't been a single time in their history when God said no to repentance. You might be far removed from God as you read this book, wondering if He will take you back, but I want to tell you He will if you will turn to Him. It will be His joy to begin again with you. It doesn't matter where you've been, you can come back. If you're sincere before God, He will restore you just as He did these people. By the time we get to the end of the book, these folks will have walked with God for quite some time. So can you!

Chapter 12

Setting Biblical Goals

Nehemiah 10

If chapters 7-9 are a record of the repentance that brings deliverance from the punishment of sin, chapter 10 is a record of the commitment required to deal with the consequences of it. True repentance before God always brings His immediate forgiveness. Yet it will require daily living for the Lord and the keeping of His ways to alleviate the consequences that are caused as a result of forsaking Him. The people with Nehemiah did not simply want to be let off the hook, they longed for God's blessing again. Nehemiah can be a difficult book to read because it doesn't leave you much room for compromise and its lessons are a constant call to let your faith in God translate into tangible behavior. It's not enough to be God's people in word, we must be so in our daily walks.

True revival will lead to changes in behavior. There are many people who verbalize perfect priorities, yet do not carry forth those priorities in their actions. When believers stray away from the Lord who saved them, it's usually caused by priorities that have been lost. It certainly was the case with Israel here. They set aside doing that which kept them close to God and, as a result, lost their will to maintain their relationship with Him.

I play golf but not very well. I believe my practice swings before I hit the ball are always perfect. Unfortunately, they don't drive the ball anywhere. So I've got to step up to the ball and actually try hitting it right, again and again. Well, that's where we find our folks in chapter 10, willing to step up again and do their best in what God has called them to do. Nehemiah describes the practical steps taken as they return to their first love.

Most of the tendency in our lives as we get older is to lose vitality, not gain it; to lose drive, to lose desire, to lose that which pushes us forward – and that is most true when it becomes a spiritual commitment. You find many quickly turning to live lives in the rear view mirror, looking back to what once was rather than forward to what God has in mind. It is, after all, far easier to look back and smile at yesterday's accomplishments than to have to look forward and face a work of faith ahead. That was what Nehemiah's generation was facing as well. There are those who believe goal-setting isn't biblical. "We just want to let the Lord do as He wants," they say. Well, so do I but we have to be headed somewhere and I believe God is a God of order and planning.

Not setting a goal only leads to spinning like a top. Here in chapter 10, the people write down some goals for themselves – difficult changes – each of which would challenge the status quo and require a greater determination on their part, as well as God's strengthening to give it their all. They addressed the things they had evidently neglected the most.

> *Now those who placed their seal on the document were:*
> *–Nehemiah 10:1a*

Verses 1 through 27 list 84 names: Nehemiah, 21 priests, 17 Levites, and 45 chiefs of tribes and overseers of areas in the government. Then we come to verse 28 …

> *Now the rest of the people — the priests, the Levites, the gatekeepers, the singers, the Nethinim, and all those who had separated themselves from the peoples of the lands to the Law of God, their wives, their sons,*

> *and their daughters, everyone who had knowledge and understanding — these joined with their brethren, their nobles, and entered into a curse and an oath to walk in God's Law, which was given by Moses the servant of God, and to observe and do all the commandments of the LORD our Lord, and His ordinances and His statutes:*
>
> *–Nehemiah 10:28-29*

This was an important day; like that day you raised your hand to receive the Lord or walked down an aisle to declare your commitment to Him. Following the example of their leaders, the people stood together in their commitment to follow God, and both accountability and encouragement would be the result. That is the role of the church today. The body of Christ is God's gift to you to help you to walk with Him, which is why in Hebrews 10:25, Paul writes: "not forsaking the assembling of ourselves together, as is the manner of some, but exhorting one another, and so much the more as you see the Day approaching." Some people erroneously believe they can maintain their relationship with God without others, but that is not a biblical truth. It is rather the deception of the enemy who seeks to isolate us so he might defeat us. Notice these made a covenant together about their home life, their social life, their business life, and their religious practices. They joined together in their devotion and so should you, in a local body, where accountability and mutual ministry can keep you heading in God's direction day by day.

> *We would not give our daughters as wives to the peoples of the land, nor take their daughters for our sons;*
>
> *–Nehemiah 10:30*

The first commitment the people made was to separate themselves from the heathens around them in terms of fellowship. In Deuteronomy 7, when Moses was rehearsing the Law to that second generation, who would soon be heading into the Promised Land with Joshua, he said, "And when the LORD your God delivers them over to you, you shall conquer them and utterly destroy them. You shall make no covenant with them nor show mercy to them" (Deuteronomy 7:2).

This had nothing to do with elitism or a "holier-than-thou" attitude and everything to do with separating themselves from the way of the world in order to follow the ways of the Lord. The people here were determined to keep their commitment to God pure. When Moses spoke to the people in Exodus 34:12, he said, "Take heed to yourself, lest you make a covenant with the inhabitants of the land where you are going, lest it be a snare in your midst." Literally, "they trap you through relationships and it damages your relationship with God." In Numbers 33:55, Moses again warned, "But if you do not drive out the inhabitants of the land from before you, then it shall be that those whom you let remain shall be irritants in your eyes and thorns in your sides, and they shall harass you in the land where you dwell." Separation is a biblical principle. Though we are called to go out into all the world to preach His Word, we are not called to seek fellowship, support, or comfort in the world. The church is for all of that, the world is for ministry and outreach.

Paul told the Corinthians, "Do not be unequally yoked together with unbelievers. For what fellowship has righteousness with lawlessness? And what communion has light with darkness? And what accord has Christ with Belial? Or what part has a believer with an unbeliever?" (2 Corinthians 6:14-15). It's not because you're better than those in the world or smarter, but because you've been called to live differently, to live for God. You've been called to walk with God and be a light to the world.

If we as saints are mostly surrounded by the unsaved and seek friendship with the world, we can quickly lose our dedication to the things of God, as these with Nehemiah had. There's no way we can go in both directions. Solomon learned this the hard way. We read of him in 1 Kings 11:4 that when he was older his wives turned his heart after other gods and his heart was no longer loyal to the Lord. He was influenced rather than being an influence. It was as Peter stood by the enemy's fires that he was able to deny the Lord in John 18. No wonder the first sermon he preached ended with the words, "Be saved from this perverse generation" (Acts 2:40).

One day, there will be a final separation, as Jesus taught in the parable of the tares (Matthew 13). Until then, we are called to separate ourselves, as these with Nehemiah were doing now in their hunger for God and His blessing.

> *if the peoples of the land brought wares or any grain to sell on the Sabbath day, we would not buy it from them on the Sabbath, or on a holy day; and we would forego the seventh year's produce and the exacting of every debt.*
>
> *–Nehemiah 10:31*

God had made a covenant with Israel in Exodus 31 that was only five verses long (Exodus 31:13-17). The laws that came out of it were man-made. It said the Sabbath would be a day of rest from your labors. It would be a day devoid of work or seeking gain, a day to recognize, worship, and honor the Lord who cared for them. Symbolically the Sabbath declared: If you never have time for God, you will die. Later the Sabbath became a type of the rest Jesus would give every man who would stop trying to work his own way to heaven (Hebrews 4:1-11).

The Old Testament law of the Sabbath applied to the land as well. You can find it in Leviticus 25, which basically said that for six years Israel could plant crops on the land, but every seventh year, nothing was to be planted in order to give the land a rest. God would see to it that the harvest of the sixth year would last through the seventh. Every 50th year, called the Year of Jubilee, there would be two years in a row where people were not to plant crops and would be sustained by the harvest of the prior year. In addition, all debts were canceled every 50 years, making the Year of Jubilee a time of great personal loss for some, but great spiritual gain for all.

Yet historically, for 490 years, the people ignored the land's Sabbath rest. When the Lord sent them into captivity because of their idolatry, He told them in 2 Chronicles 36 that they would remain in Babylon for 70 years as payment for the years they had failed to observe the law of the land's Sabbath rest. Here in Nehemiah, in this time of repentance and revival, the people said, "We will let the land rest. We will not collect our debts. We'll keep the year of Jubilee." It was going to cost them to put God first but they had learned they could afford nothing less.

> *Also we made ordinances for ourselves, to exact from ourselves yearly one-third of a shekel for the service of the house of our God: for the showbread, for the regular grain offering, for the regular burnt offering of the Sabbaths, the New Moons, and the set feasts; for the holy things, for the sin offerings to make atonement for Israel, and all the work of the house of our God. We cast lots among the priests, the Levites, and the people, for bringing the wood offering into the house of our God, according to our fathers' houses, at the appointed times year by year, to burn on the altar of the LORD our God as it is written in the Law.*
>
> *–Nehemiah 10:32-34*

Their giving to the things of God, or their investment in their spiritual well-being, was restored. "A fire shall always be burning on the altar; it shall never go out," the Lord declared in Leviticus 6:13. This place of sacrifice speaks of the access that we can have to the Lord and His willingness to hear from His people. But to keep the fire going continually, to lay the burnt offering upon it every morning, and to burn the fat of the peace offering upon it, came with a cost and an ongoing committed effort on their part. Here the priests and all of the people cast lots (an Old Testament method by which God made His will known) to take responsibility to provide wood for that fire to continue without interruption. We will see in chapter 13 that Nehemiah also took part. No one could do this work by himself, no one could afford to, but together they could accomplish it. We need the body! For some folks, this may have been a huge burden. But if you're hungry to be right with God, having set Him aside for too long, you soon realize that the burdens you are carrying for failing to serve Him are far greater than the ones you'll have to undertake to do things His way. So they decided together, let's do it His way!

> *And we made ordinances to bring the firstfruits of our ground and the firstfruits of all fruit of all trees, year by year, to the house of the LORD; to bring the first-born of our sons and our cattle, as it is written in the Law, and the firstborn of our herds and our flocks, to the house of our God, to the priests who minister in the house of our God; to bring the firstfruits of our dough, our offerings, the fruit from all kinds of trees, the new wine and oil, to the priests, to the storerooms of the house of our God; and to bring the tithes of our land to the Levites, for the Levites should receive the tithes in all our farming communities. And the priest, the descendant of Aaron, shall be with the Levites when the Levites receive tithes; and the Levites shall bring up a tenth of the tithes to the house of our God, to the rooms of the storehouse.*
>
> *–Nehemiah 10:35-38*

According to the Old Testament law, God's people had an obligation to maintain the temple, the place of meeting between God and man. This meant employing the priests so they could do their daily devotions, offer sacrifices, and be available to the people. Here they make a huge commitment to bring a tenth of their increase in order to invest in their spiritual well-being by supporting the priests. It is quite a step from people who were living under heavy taxation and tremendous poverty. Yet the overriding principle is the same: first things first. They wanted to get rid of the consequences of not following God, and though it would be difficult to do, it was the only way to right the ship.

It is extremely difficult to start giving in a time when you don't have much to give and after you've neglected the practice for so long that you really don't see how there could be any benefit to doing so. Yet the Bible teaches that everything we have is God's anyway. In the book of Haggai, we read that when the people were supposed to be building the temple, they chose instead to build their own houses first. For a dozen years they set aside work on the temple. When Haggai arrived, he had a mouthful of mad from the Lord. One of the things he asked them was: "'Is it time for you yourselves to dwell in your paneled houses, and this temple to lie in ruins?' Now therefore, thus says the LORD of hosts: 'Consider your ways! You have sown much, and bring in little; You eat, but do not have enough; You drink, but you are not filled with drink; You clothe yourselves, but no one is warm; And he who earns wages, Earns wages to put into a bag with holes'" (Haggai 1:4-6).

By the time Nehemiah arrived, the people had learned their lesson. There was a general willingness among them to be good stewards of the work of God. But it wouldn't come without sacrifice.

I find this to be true in the local church. Everything physical depends upon the tithing and the giving of the people – from every tract to every light bulb. Yet balancing that is Jesus' promise that He will build His church and the gates of hell won't prevail against it (Matthew 16:18). So, on one hand, we have a responsibility, and onn the other hand, our trust is not in that. Our trust is in God's provision because God never fails.

I look at these families with Nehemiah who are in such desperate need and I realize it is only as they came to love God that they were able to make this step, despite the dire circumstances, which I find is often the case. When God truly gets your heart, He will get hold of your pocketbook as well. Scripture bears this out, as in Exodus 25 through 36, where we are told about the building of the tabernacle in the wilderness using materials the people were invited to willingly contribute. Eventually you read of the construction crew coming to Moses and saying, "Tell the people to quit giving. We've got way more than we need!" That's something I've never heard from radio or television preachers. I hear, "Summer's tough for us. Can you give a little bit more?" I never hear, "We've got plenty." Ever. But wouldn't that be great to hear?

In Ezra 1-2 as some 50,000 were preparing to return to Jerusalem from Babylon, Ezra essentially told them, "If you want to give to help us build the temple, do so. But otherwise, don't worry about it." And the people gave so much as a result of their hearts being turned to the Lord that he was afraid to travel with it! When David, in 1 Chronicles 29, gathered the people to talk to them about the temple he wanted to build, the resources were plenty because the Lord had moved their hearts. Solomon wrote in Ecclesiastes 5:13, "There is a severe evil which I have seen under the sun: Riches kept for their owner to his hurt." Self-interest drives you when your heart is caught up in the world. Love and selflessness motivates the heart surrendered to the Lord.

Loving God should be the issue, not giving. In 2 Corinthians 9, Paul wrote about us giving with a willing mind, about planning beforehand what you're going to give so that when you arrived, no one's appeals would sway what God had placed on your heart. He talked about giving "hilariously," according to your ability. Does God need you to give? Absolutely not. Do you need to give because it is a reflection of your love? Absolutely so. "Freely you have received, freely give," Jesus said (Matthew 10:8). There is a direct connection indeed.

There are even Scriptures that talk about robbing God by not giving, which He told us will lead to chastisement and the curse that comes from withholding from Him (Malachi 3:8-9). Those verses are not given as a motivation but rather as a warning. God gives us plenty of encouragement, but here is the principle most often repeated: People who love God support and invest themselves in those things that benefit His kingdom because that is their greatest interest.

Practically speaking, some 45 percent of the people who attend our church never give. That means 55 percent support the 100 percent who come. Is that OK? It's OK with me because God has always provided for every need we've ever had. We're not in debt. The building is paid for. We don't buy things and hope to pay for them later. If the Lord provides, we'll buy it. If He doesn't, we won't. There's no "buying by faith." That's called stupid, but trusting God isn't. He hasn't failed us once.

So the vows of the people in Jerusalem here in our verses came from hearts that had been moved by Him. They joined together to repent of their sins. They committed themselves to forsaking their self-interest and to instead seek that which mattered to God. They separated themselves from a worldly lifestyle and from worldly people when it came to marriage, fellowship, and commerce. When the world came to offer them Sabbath day sales, they said, "No, thank you." They committed themselves to observing the Year of Jubilee. In short, they chose to seek the kingdom of God and His righteousness (Matthew 6:33).

Breaking free from the worldly magnet that had drawn them so hard and so long was a big step and a difficult process. But the difference now was that they knew it was worth the cost and they were tired of what they had been getting.

It's all about priorities, isn't it? You should run everything you do – the way you work, how you spend your time, how you spend your resources, your relationships with others

– through the filter of Matthew 6:33: "But seek first the kingdom of God and His righteousness, and all these things shall be added to you."

The ball is in your court.

Chapter 13

A Place For All, And All In Their Places

Nehemiah 11

Chapter 11 is the final chapter recording the revival that took place in Jerusalem following the completion of the wall. It is an interesting chapter for it is filled with names and places, along with things people did and didn't do. It sets before us a tremendous example of what God can do when people listen to Him. It is a picture not only of the faithfulness that people showed to the Lord, but of His ability to know every individual that was involved in His work. It is a chapter that will assure you that if you serve the Lord, He will remember. People might not know you, kindnesses may be forgotten, or faithful sacrifices overlooked, but not by our Lord. In truth, if He is doing a work in your life and you've committed yourself to Him, that's really all you need to know; that He sees, He knows, and He will remember (Hebrews 6:10). The bottom line, the ultimate line for us as believers, is that we seek to please our Lord who knows all.

> *Now the leaders of the people dwelt at Jerusalem; the rest of the people cast lots to bring one out of ten to dwell in Jerusalem, the holy city, and nine-tenths were to dwell in other cities. And the people blessed all the men who willingly offered themselves to dwell at Jerusalem.*
>
> *–Nehemiah 11:1-2*

Though the walls were up, the city of Jerusalem itself still looked and felt like a ghost town. It was large and spacious, but it had no businesses, no industry, and no jobs. You couldn't go to the corner market for your necessities. There was no one in the city able to provide you with animals for sacrifice or food for your table. To move yourself or your family into the city behind its walls would have brought great difficulty and demanded great sacrifice.

Yet without the pioneering heart of some, Jerusalem would never again be filled with people or be vibrant in its witness to its God. That is the challenge that Nehemiah and the people now faced. I imagine that the Jerusalem Chamber of Commerce had a hard time selling these houses: cheap land, lots of rocks. It wasn't exactly a very appealing offer. Yet both the leaders and those who followed them joined together to continue to serve the Lord at great personal cost.

We read in verse 1 that the leaders themselves did what they asked of others, which is a novel idea considering the kind of leadership that we are accustomed to dealing with in this day and age. They practiced what they preached. They moved themselves into town, leaving their homes and communities, to live in this rugged place where there was nothing for them besides the glorious promise and work of God amongst them.

Following the example of their leaders, the people cast lots to determine who should then move to Jerusalem as well. Casting lots sounds like a dice game, but in the Old Testament, it was one of the ways which the Lord gave the priests to determine His will. Proverbs 16:33 says, "The lot is cast into the lap, But its every decision is from the LORD." Often you will read that when the people were willing to hear from God, He would speak to them through this manner. In the New Testament, after the Holy Spirit was given to dwell in man, you no longer find this practice. But before that time, it was one of the methods through which God would make His will known. The important thing to learn here is that the thousands who lived in and around Jerusalem at this time were all interested in knowing what God wanted and were willing to do what He said.

As the lot was cast, 10 percent of the people were marked by the Lord to leave their place of comfort and go to a place of difficulty for the benefit of all. And they did it! According to verse 2, the people blessed these willing servants and honored the Lord who moved upon their hearts. Even though 10 percent were mandated and were obedient, there were others, it seems, who willingly joined in the work and moved into the city. I love the word "willing" here. It could be translated: to be incited from within. It means you make a choice not based on the pressure from without or from the suggestion of others, but solely upon what God is doing in your heart. So there were some who just wanted to be a part of God's work. They were willing to pull up their roots and take bold steps of faith.

Part of the sin of the people previously was that they had forsaken working on the temple in order to build their own homes. So I'm assuming some of these families lived in some pretty nice places, but they were going to leave behind all of the goods they had gathered upon the earth, in order to put the Lord first.

I equate these servants with our missionaries today who leave the comfort of home behind in order to preach Jesus in difficult places around the world. Like the people who blessed the pioneers in Nehemiah's day, I so greatly admire the calling and faithfulness of men and women who leave it all behind for His glory.

Beginning in verse 3, we are given a list of names and various groups who moved into Jerusalem. Primarily they are from the tribes of Judah and Benjamin because when Joshua was doling out the land by God's direction years earlier, it was these two tribes who were given the area surrounding Jerusalem. So in verses 3-9 they are mentioned, some by name, others by number. A total of 1,396 souls from Judah and Benjamin moved in and made that commitment to go into Jerusalem to establish life in the city.

In verses 10-14, there is a list of 1,192 priests and their families who were specifically involved in the service, worship, and sacrifices at the temple. There were a lot of people serving at the place of worship. I love all of those who serve in our body here at Morningstar and do so year in and year out seeking to love God's people. At the end of verse 16, we also read of those believers who were ministering to the Lord living and laboring in the secular world. The insurance agent, the real estate salesman, the finance manager, the doctor, the dentist, the person who filled out purchase orders – they were overseen by the Levites outside of the wall; they had secular jobs, but they weren't secular people.

In verses 17-18, we read of two descendants of Asaph and Jeduthun who were involved in the ministry of prayer and worship. Years earlier, as David was gathering materials for his son Solomon to build the temple, he also organized and established the worship teams who would lead the people in worship when the temple was finished and functional. Asaph and Jeduthun worked with David then, and here we see their descendants taking part in the same areas of ministry years later.

In verse 19, we read that there were 172 men who served to protect the people. Two men named Akkub and Talmon were two overseers responsible for the gatekeepers. Praise the Lord they took their positions.

In verse 22, the overseer was a fellow named Uzzi. "Uzzi" in Hebrew means "strong." Then, we are told in verse 23 that it was by the king's command that a certain portion of financial support had been set aside for the singers and the worship leaders. We read in Ezra 7, when Ezra had come 12 years earlier, that Artaxerxes, the Medo-Persian king, had given tax-free status to those who returned to re-inhabit Jerusalem. Here we learn he was also apparently subsidizing some of the work in and around Jerusalem, work which couldn't have been funded on its own due to the lack of industry and economic stability. So God used this king to help finance His work, similar to the tax-free status given to the church today. God faithfully provides for each of us.

From verse 25 to the end of the chapter, we are given a list of some of the places those from Judah and Benjamin would call home. These were those who didn't move into town but instead moved down the street, down the block, or many miles away. These places included Lachish to the north and Beersheba to the south. They began to plant themselves in and around Jerusalem as they became that community and extended community. They had their own challenges. However, living outside of town had some great advantages: the roads would have been in, the industries would have been available, and the farming was already taking place. They could probably live a little more comfortably and without having to live behind a wall. But they would be exposed to marauding armies because they weren't established. Look over the names, how many do you recognize? They were farmers. They raised crops for food and trade. They raised animals for sacrifice and were as vital to this part of the work as anyone else.

By the time you arrive at the end of this report here in chapter 11, you can't help but conclude and realize that God's heart is always about working through the many, not just the few; all, not some, are needed as God works in us and through us. It is a truth repeated throughout the Scriptures culminating in the picture of the church as one body with so many parts. The work of the church includes those who are Christians in business outside the wall, so to speak, for the benefit of others. Others work within the church. But notice that wherever these people were called, they went and they were all equally useful to God's plan. You couldn't have survived in Jerusalem without the saints in the villages. You couldn't survive in the village without the folks in Jerusalem. There was a real inter-dependency. Whether you were on the front lines or way to the rear, everyone worked together and that is the key. The only prerequisite was faithfulness to one's calling.

I don't doubt that God put this chapter in here just to convince us that He is well aware of our service to Him. All of you would recognize Billy Graham's name, but I doubt you know the name of his finance minister, or the guy who did his international organizations for years, or the folks who went six months ahead and set up things in different coliseums and stadiums. You don't know them but God does. Here in chapter 11 are other people you don't know. You won't find them anywhere else in the Bible. They are far less known than Nehemiah or Ezra – yet their callings were absolutely as vital.

Chapter 11 becomes a list of nobodies whom God used because they are all somebody in His eyes, in His plan, and in His work. They're the MASH units on the front line. They're the linemen who block for the well-known quarterback or running back. They're deserving of recognition. So God recognizes them and He puts their names here in what would otherwise seem to be a throwaway chapter. Here God is saying in the midst of the revival, "Look what all of these people did to be a part of My work." As we mentioned earlier from Hebrews 6:10, it bears repeating: "For God is not unjust to forget your work and labor of love which you have shown toward His name, in that you have ministered to the saints, and do minister." God knows those who are faithful to Him. If you were to visit Arlington National Cemetery and walk through the rows of white crosses you find there, they would represent to you very unfamiliar people. Unless you're looking for someone by name, you really have no idea who those crosses represent – except that every cross stands for an extraordinary sacrifice someone made so that you could worship freely today. You didn't shed a tear over their deaths as others have, but you have benefited from their lives.

From an application standpoint, I think the reason we, as Christians, find difficulty in placing ourselves in the service of the Lord in church is that we battle with something we falsely learned in the world: that honor, recognition, and acknowledgment ought to be a part of anything we do. So if that's not available to me, then it must not be the Lord. But I would suggest to you that most of these folks weren't applauded by anyone. Had the Lord not written about it, we would have no history of their work at all. In reality, any call of God to a place of service that is in the background usually meets with the resistance of our flesh.

Do you realize that your physical well-being depends upon organs that you never see? You can get along without an ear. You can lose a finger. You can lose a hand, an arm, or a leg. There's a lot of stuff that can fall off and you can keep going. But if you try getting along without your brain or your lungs or your heart, you're dead. You are dependent upon the unseen, aren't you? That's the way ministry is, too. Most ministry has significance because of the unseen. We don't know any of these names. We can't track them down, but God did. You may not serve in a place where you find much applause, thanks, or acknowledgment, but God sees. If you please Him, you've done what you're supposed to with your life. The key is, where does God want you to serve? It may be in a place where you're not seen. Love for the Lord drove these people to serve in anonymity and will drive you as well. Paul wrote to the Ephesians, "Bondservants, be obedient to those who are your masters according to the flesh, with fear and trembling, in sincerity of heart, as to Christ; not with eyeservice, as men-pleasers, but as bondservants of Christ, doing the will of God from the heart, with goodwill doing service, as to the Lord, and not to men, knowing that whatever good anyone does, he will receive the same from the Lord, whether he is a slave or free" (Ephesians 6:5-8). Do the will of God from your heart and know this: any good that comes from it, you'll receive a reward from the Lord. In other words, let God be your motivation in what you choose to do and where you choose to serve.

As part of the body of Christ, we can learn a lot from their example: the value of the part contributing to the whole, the value of finding the place God has put you, the right motivation to serve, the importance of leadership example, and the need to minister to others. Here in the midst of revival, everyone found their place from the Lord and served from there willingly. They were interested only in pleasing Him as we see them taking some of the lowliest, most difficult, and least-appreciated spots you could find. Jesus warned His disciples in Matthew 6:1, "Take heed that you do not do your charitable deeds before men, to be seen by them. Otherwise you have no reward from your Father in heaven." If you hear men's applause, there goes your reward. "Oh, you're so great. You're so wonderful. Thank you so much." Poof! But God keeps great track of hearts that are serving the Lord.

I don't know what God has in store for you, but I do know what God hasn't called you to do, and that is to sit idly by. When the Spirit of God begins to move, people find their place and begin to serve. The benefit is not just to them or to those around them but to the church as a whole. The testimony of the church in the eyes of the world stands out. We can't do it alone, we have to do it together.

The question is, where are you going to serve? Where is your Nehemiah 11 spot?

Chapter 14

Joy On The Wall

Nehemiah 12

Chapter 12 is a record of the dedication of the wall and a recording of people filled with great joy. Now that the people's hearts are right with God, they wanted to go back to the wall that had been built and say, "God did this. Let's honor Him with it." And they gathered with great joy around it. I find it very interesting that Nehemiah would spend an entire chapter committed to the dedication of the wall.

If joy were a disease, I'm sure it would be listed as extremely contagious. You'd probably have to wear a mask or something. People with real joy are always in demand, they're fun to be around. If you've been around people who are always joyful, you know what I mean. The world certainly doesn't promote being joyful. We have 24-hour news to depress ourselves at any hour of the day. The bleak forecast, the political circus, the uncertain times, wars and rumors of wars, terrorism, and the economy – there's more than enough to steal your joy. Yet from everything I've read in the Bible, God's desire is that we would be filled with joy, and not just on Sunday morning for an hour, or on Thanksgiving weekend when you might get a day or two off at work, but every day, in all situations, at all times, in all circumstances.

God's joy is a joy that will lighten the burden you carry in this life. It is a joy that comes from seeing life from His point of view. It's not an, "I'll bury my head in the sand and pretend there's nothing wrong" kind of fake joy. It is rather the assurance that these with Nehemiah finally came to know – God is with us. These were poor people that were often threatened and lived in the midst of enemies. The king wasn't always going to be their friend. There was really nothing they could point to that was good outwardly other than that they finally had erected a wall. But something great had happened to them because they learned just as Nehemiah, Ezra, and all of the priests had, that there was a God they could serve who was worth waiting upon and depending upon, who would come through for them, and would be their Lord.

That's the story of chapter 12. It is the spontaneous overflow of joy coming from a people who finally were convinced that God was in their midst and they were seeing their lives through His eyes.

The first 26 verses found here is a list of the genealogy of the priests and Levites who had left Babylon with Zerubbabel and Joshua 91 years earlier to come to Jerusalem to rebuild the city and the temple. These were the forefathers of those who, two and three generations later, would now gather on the walls to praise the Lord in 445 BC.

So, led by the Spirit, Nehemiah focuses on this dedication and especially the joy accompanying it. In fact, he mentions the words "joy" and "rejoicing" so much you can't help but notice he is overcome with it! He simply wants to express that overwhelming joy that comes when the work of God is found in the lives of people who have dedicated their lives to Him.

Joy is always a by-product. If you're not joyful today, it can probably be traced back to the fact that you're not looking at life from God's perspective and you do not really believe what He has to say, because if you made a list of everything He's promised to do, you'd be very joyful indeed.

Let's jump ahead to verse 27 …

> *Now at the dedication of the wall of Jerusalem they sought out the Levites in all their places, to bring them*

to Jerusalem to celebrate the dedication with gladness, both with thanksgivings and singing, with cymbals and stringed instruments and harps. And the sons of the singers gathered together from the countryside around Jerusalem, from the villages of the Netophathites, from the house of Gilgal, and from the fields of Geba and Azmaveth; for the singers had built themselves villages all around Jerusalem.

–Nehemiah 12:27-29

I find it enlightening and instructive that as God began to work in the hearts of the people, those who served in ministry soon sought to move closer to the work. They put themselves in a position to be available for service at a moment's notice. Here the invitations went out to the worship leaders, the Levites, the singers, and the priests. Everyone was invited to come and celebrate. Let's get together for a party in His honor!

Then the priests and Levites purified themselves, and purified the people, the gates, and the wall.

–Nehemiah 12:30

From an Old Testament viewpoint, ceremonial purification always speaks of commitment to God and was to be performed before any religious activity. It addressed the heart and the outlook of the would-be worshiper. Are you going to walk with God? Is this going to be a part of your life? Are you doing this because your heart is right with Him or just out of a sense of obligation? The purification was to bring this to the surface.

For years, ceremonial cleansing had been done arbitrarily, but these had been touched by God. So for the first time in a long time, they took seriously their commitment to the Lord and truly examined their hearts.

We're not told how they did this. We don't know if

they prayed over the wall or anointed it with oil, but we do know that holiness always precedes joy. You can only find the joy of the Lord in a life set aside for His use. You're going to have to commit yourself to the Lord once and for all. Here, for the first time in hundreds of years, God became the center of the national life of His people again.

The priests dedicated themselves, the people, the gates, and the wall itself. And in so doing, they said, "God, it's all Yours. You did this. We're blown away by what You've done."

> *So I brought the leaders of Judah up on the wall, and appointed two large thanksgiving choirs. One went to the right hand on the wall toward the Refuse Gate. After them went Hoshaiah and half of the leaders of Judah, and Azariah, Ezra, Meshullam, Judah, Benjamin, Shemaiah, Jeremiah, and some of the priests' sons with trumpets – Zechariah the son of Jonathan, the son of Shemaiah, the son of Mattaniah, the son of Michaiah, the son of Zaccur, the son of Asaph, and his brethren, Shemaiah, Azarel, Milalai, Gilalai, Maai, Nethanel, Judah, and Hanani, with the musical instruments of David the man of God. Ezra the scribe went before them. By the Fountain Gate, in front of them, they went up the stairs of the City of David, on the stairway of the wall, beyond the house of David, as far as the Water Gate eastward. The other thanksgiving choir went the opposite way, and I was behind them with half of the people on the wall, going past the Tower of the Ovens as far as the Broad Wall, and above the Gate of Ephraim, above the Old Gate, above the Fish Gate, the Tower of Hananel, the Tower of the Hundred, as far as the Sheep Gate; and they stopped by the Gate of the Prison.*
>
> *–Nehemiah 12:31-39*

The Jerusalem wall was about 12 feet thick, so from the gates that are mentioned here and how far they went in every direction, it is easily and conservatively estimated that there were 5 to 10 thousand people standing on the wall itself. Of these, Nehemiah organized two choirs. Half of the singers went one direction with Ezra and the other half went in the other direction with him.

This wasn't some solemn tight-lipped occasion, this was more like a parade. Songs were being sung, music was playing, and many were standing on the wall by the grace of God. It's such a great picture of outward enthusiasm as thousands showed up – not driven by hype or hysteria generated by some good manipulators, but out of a sincere response to the goodness of God from the hearts of a grateful people.

> *So the two thanksgiving choirs stood in the house of God, likewise I and the half of the rulers with me; and the priests, Eliakim, Maaseiah, Minjamin, Michaiah, Elioenai, Zechariah, and Hananiah, with trumpets; also Maaseiah, Shemaiah, Eleazar, Uzzi, Jehohanan, Malchijah, Elam, and Ezer. The singers sang loudly with Jezrahiah the director. Also that day they offered great sacrifices, and rejoiced, for God had made them rejoice with great joy; the women and the children also rejoiced, so that the joy of Jerusalem was heard afar off.*
>
> *–Nehemiah 12:40-43*

The house of God, the place where He dwells, should be filled with joy. Do you think you're going to get to heaven one day and look around and see a bunch of people with long faces because it's "Moody Monday"? No! According to Psalm 16:11, there's going to be great joy in God's presence – a fullness of joy. That's what God wants for us, but you can't make joy your goal. It has to be a by-product of something else. You can't determine to put a smile on your face and be joyful all day. Your best bet if you're going to make joy your goal is to stay in bed. And even then, something is going to irritate you. Joy has to be the result of something else. For these people, the joy that filled their hearts, according to what you read in chapters 7-11, was the dedication of their lives to God and doing things the way God intended them to be done, sometimes even at tremendous cost to themselves. Through that, they found His awesome blessings upon them.

Can you hear these choirs singing back and forth at the top of their lungs? There were three-part harmonies, a guys' part and a girls' part. You could be a long ways off and hear what was going on. If you've ever shown up late for a baseball or football game, you know that the noise from the stadium will make you move quicker. We're missing out! Let's go! I imagine that was the case outside Jerusalem that day.

The word "joy" is used 5 times in verse 43 alone simply to describe the demeanor of the people of God that day. It was a joy that touched moms, dads, kids, and neighborhoods; it was a joy that was expressed in family and fellowship, and that was celebratory. It was a genuine revival!

> *And at the same time some were appointed over the rooms of the storehouse for the offerings, the firstfruits, and the tithes, to gather into them from the fields of the cities the portions specified by the Law for the priests and Levites; for Judah rejoiced over the priests and Levites who ministered. Both the singers and the gatekeepers kept the charge of their God and the charge of the purification, according to the command of David and Solomon his son. For in the days of David and Asaph of old there were chiefs of the singers, and songs of praise and thanksgiving to God. In the days of Zerubbabel and in the days of Nehemiah all Israel gave the portions for the singers and the gatekeepers, a portion for each day. They also consecrated holy things for the Levites, and the Levites consecrated them for the chil-*

dren of Aaron.

–Nehemiah 12:44-47

There was joy in singing. There was joy in serving. There was even joy in giving. The commitments were made as a result of joy and that joy came from doing things the way God had said. They had been obeying the Lord and it was beginning to show. People were giving with joy! Their giving had enabled the priests and singers to return to their calling of serving the Lord at the temple and it blessed the nation as a whole.

In fact, in writing, Nehemiah reaches back 400-plus years to the days of David, when the nation had professional worship leaders like Asaph, who could spend their time doing things to serve the people. In the days of Zerubbabel, only 91 years earlier, the same was true. And here, in the days of Nehemiah, God was again stirring the hearts of the people. They were able to support His work with great joy.

I love this chapter because it teaches us that being spiritual doesn't mean you have to be somber. God's will is that you rejoice. Christians who are disappointed or frustrated, who walk around with a cloud over their head, stopped looking at life from God's point of view. They had lost God-vision! Other outlooks and goals clouded their view.

The world's joy is defined by emotional feelings that are dependent upon favorable circumstances. You are going to need a couple of good breaks if you're going to have even a moment's worth of joy because there's very little in your control. You can't control the weather. You can't control your health. You can take care of yourself and still die on the treadmill of a heart attack while drinking that protein shake with vitamins in your hand. Your best bet is to say, "I'm going to have whatever God has for me. And because He is good and because He is for me, I can face even the most difficult things knowing He is with me." That may not be the easiest position to take, but what alternative do you have? Only the joy that comes from knowing God is permanent.

Worldly joy is tenuous and it changes with the situation. Heavenly joy is a fruit of the Holy Spirit. It is not affected by outward circumstance and it never changes because God doesn't change. His plan for you today is what it was yesterday and what it will be tomorrow. You won't wake up and find God in a bad mood. You'll never hear Him say, "I know what I told you yesterday, but I had a whole night to think about it and having discussed it with the Holy Spirit we've come up with a different idea." No, He is the same yesterday, today, and forever and you can count on that!

That's what these people had come to understand. "You have put gladness in my heart, More than in the season that their grain and wine increased," the psalmist declares in Psalm 4:7. God's joy is far superior to anything you can receive from the world, to any temporary gain you might lay your hands on. But God's joy can overflow even at the worst of times.

"…I am exceedingly joyful in all our tribulation," Paul wrote in 2 Corinthians 7:4. People will think you have lost your mind if you say, "I've really been going through it and I couldn't be more happy about it." It doesn't make any sense unless the Lord is your Lord and you're convinced of His ways and of His Word. Our trials must first pass through the Lord's desk and get His approval. If He allows them, He does so in love, with reason, and for our benefit. Knowing that our joy is real and established, the world will take notice, because it is so uncommon in the world.

Writing about the conditions of the days in which he lived, Habakkuk began by complaining to the Lord, "O LORD, how long shall I cry, And You will not hear? Even cry out to You, 'Violence!' And You will not save. Why do You show me iniquity, And cause me to see trouble? For plundering and violence are before me; There is strife, and contention arises" (Habakkuk 1:2-3). "I don't want to see any more of this because You're obviously not concerned at all about it," exclaimed the prophet. "The wicked surround the righteous.

Justice never goes forth. The Law is powerless. There is a perversion in judgment. The wicked are in control. I've had it." The Lord's response to Habakkuk was basically this: "May be you should look at life from what I'm doing rather than from what you see, because I am doing a work and if I told you, you wouldn't believe Me." When the Lord did tell him what He was doing, Habakkuk indeed said, "I don't believe it." Three chapters later in his little prophetic book, nothing had outwardly changed, but something had happened to the prophet. This same man who was griping and complaining in Habakkuk 1 is now singing a different tune altogether. Listen to what he proclaims in Habakkuk 3:17-19: "Though the fig tree may not blossom, Nor fruit be on the vines; Though the labor of the olive may fail, And the fields yield no food; Though the flock may be cut off from the fold, And there be no herd in the stalls— Yet I will rejoice in the LORD, I will joy in the God of my salvation. The LORD God is my strength; He will make my feet like deer's feet, And He will make me walk on my high hills. To the Chief Musician. With my stringed instruments."

Nothing had changed except Habakkuk's outlook and understanding of the heart of God. If you're not filled with joy right now, don't blame God. He's got it all figured out. You come around to His way of thinking, sit on His side of the desk, look at your situation from His vantage point, and you'll find great joy in His love, goodness, and purpose for your life. That's what you find here with Nehemiah and God's people.

If God fills us with joy, who can steal that from us? It's only when we balk, when we don't believe Him, and when we don't rest in Him that we've got problems. Paul shares this prayer with the church in Rome: "Now may the God of hope fill you with all joy and peace in believing, that you may abound in hope by the power of the Holy Spirit" (Romans 15:13). That's my prayer for you as well.

In John 17:13, Jesus prayed for the saints who would believe in Him and says, "But now I come to You, and these things I speak in the world, that they may have My joy fulfilled in themselves." What a great prayer! You find that kind of joy being fulfilled here on the wall as well.

The secret of joy, though it is not a very well-kept secret, is that fellowship with God through prayer, worship, obedience, study, and service will fill a heart with His joy. It doesn't matter how difficult life is, God is still on the throne so I can rest. Does that mean in the world you won't have tribulation? No. Does that mean you won't have to go out and sow with tears? No. But you'll come back reaping with joy. The end result will be that God will have His way and you are blessed seeking Him.

I think about Paul in a Roman jail cell awaiting the results of his capital punishment trial. He had no idea what Nero might decide. As he sits day after day in a scary and depressing place, he feels led to write a book about joy. Really? From death row? Indeed from there Paul wrote his famous letter to the Philippians. At a time where every noise coming down the hallway towards his cell could be the executioner coming for him, Paul sits down to write about the great joy in the Lord that he had. Here is one memory verse from that letter: "Rejoice in the Lord always. Again I will say, rejoice!" (Philippians 4:4).

The night Jesus was to be betrayed He told His disciples, "Most assuredly, I say to you that you will weep and lament, but the world will rejoice; and you will be sorrowful, but your sorrow will be turned into joy" (John 16:20). He was referring to the next 3 days, when they thought He was gone and the world thought it had won over Him. He compared their sorrow and anguish to a woman giving birth. It was a painful process for the mother, but she will effectively forget all about the pain involved once she looks into the eyes of that beautiful baby born to her. That's how sorrow is turned to joy. God will use our circumstances, as difficult as they might be, to draw us near so we know Him better, see Him more clearly, and then our joy will be found in that knowledge of His goodness and love.

Paul and Silas were arrested in Philippi and beaten for their faith. In Acts 16, you can read of them being tossed into the lowest parts of the prison. Sitting back to back, chained to the ground, bloody and bruised, we find them doing the unthinkable; they were singing worship songs with joy. "But at midnight Paul and Silas were praying and singing hymns to God, and the prisoners were listening to them" (Acts 16:25). These are crazy people indeed, these Christians. It's hard to stop crazy people who are filled with joy.

Jeremiah lived at a time when joy could easily have escaped him. In his ministry he preached for over 50 years and no one ever listened or responded to his message. But that didn't stop him from writing, "Your words were found, and I ate them, And Your word was to me the joy and rejoicing of my heart; For I am called by Your name, O LORD God of hosts" (Jeremiah 15:16).

That's what happened here on the wall; people found God's joy. We learned a few chapters earlier that due to the abuse of a few, many families were facing insurmountable debt and might do so for the rest of their lives. That had not changed. Many of their challenges were still challenges. The only thing that had changed was their attitude towards God and their understanding of His goodness and love. It produced in them a joy unspeakable and full of glory.

If Christians can't find a reason to rejoice, then who can? Some 100 years from now, everyone in the world will have lost their joy and yours will just be starting! I think joy can be a tremendous witness to a world watching the evening news and longing for weekends to drown their sorrows. We have what they want and we know where to get it. Which is why we preach Jesus and His love, mercy, and grace.

My prayer for you is that you might walk in God's joy, sing His praises often, and be thankful. You have every reason to be grateful. You may have nothing much in terms of worldly goods, but you have heaven to go to and you have a God who watches over your every step. May you serve Him with joy, valuing the wonderful blessings He has given you. And may you be a witness to the world that there's a God who brings His people great joy.

Go stand on the wall and make some noise!

Chapter 15

Daily Diligence Needed

Nehemiah 13

Nehemiah had come to Jerusalem in the 20th year of Artaxerxes' reign. He was there for 12 years – first as the leader in the work of rebuilding the wall. After that, he was a spiritual leader, gathering people together to teach and to learn the Word of God. He also served as governor of the region, appointed by Artaxerxes. At the end of 12 years, verse 6 of this chapter tells us he returned to Babylon.

We don't know how long Nehemiah was gone from Jerusalem, but chapter 13 is a report of what happened when he came back. It is a lesson to us of how quickly things can go south when we lose good spiritual leadership and when a daily walk with God is set aside. We all need good, strong spiritual leaders to look up to and be encouraged by. We need to daily seek the Lord as there is no real way to maintain spiritual life otherwise. Maybe the best comparison is a physical one: If you stop going to the gym to work out, it won't be long before you feel as if you'd never been. Bodily exercise may profit little, as Paul wrote to Timothy (1 Timothy 4:8), but at least it profits some! How much more important is the exercise necessary for your spiritual well-being?

We are given this report of Nehemiah's return to Jerusalem after what would appear to be the passing of several years. In his absence, people had gotten married, practices had been established, and things had changed drastically. The revival we read of in chapters 6-12 had completely disappeared.

What are we supposed to learn from this? The lessons are straightforward and grieving to the soul. You can't coast your way to heaven. You've got to run and keep running the race until the Lord calls you home. There is no time off, no break in the action, no sitting on the sidelines. If we become lax in our walk with our Lord, in obedience to His Word, and if we are careless in the guarding of our hearts, we will soon find ourselves far removed from what His will is for our lives. That is what happened here. We're called to run the race to win, not sit on the bench (1 Corinthians 9:24, Hebrews 12:1). And, since much of this race is opposed by the world, we are running uphill. If you stop moving then you will slide backwards, that's a given.

Nehemiah 13 finds Nehemiah on the warpath, angry over what he finds, and determined to set the ship back on course. We could use some more Nehemiahs today!

> *On that day they read from the Book of Moses in the hearing of the people, and in it was found written that no Ammonite or Moabite should ever come into the assembly of God, because they had not met the children of Israel with bread and water, but hired Balaam against them to curse them. However, our God turned the curse into a blessing. So it was, when they had heard the Law, that they separated all the mixed multitude from Israel. Now before this, Eliashib the priest, having authority over the storerooms of the house of our God, was allied with Tobiah. And he had prepared for him a large room, where previously they had stored the grain offerings, the frankincense, the articles, the tithes of grain, the new wine and oil, which were commanded to be given to the Levites and singers and gatekeepers, and the offerings for the priests. But during all this I was not in Jerusalem, for in the thirty-second year of Artaxerxes king of Babylon I had returned to the king.*
>
> *–Nehemiah 13:1-6a*

It is disheartening and unbelievable to realize how quickly we can stumble and fall in our spiritual lives. The devotion that had kept them early on, the changes in the culture they had affected, the risks they had taken to build the wall, the sacrifices they made to move into town, the re-establishment of temple services and sacrifices made me want to stand on the sidelines and cheer them on. They were seeking God like they hadn't in generations. This was not some forced revival by some strong-willed leader demanding spiritual reforms from them. No, everyone was thrilled about what God was doing. It was true revival in the hearts of the people. They had returned to the Word on their own, repented of their sin, and made a new covenant with God. But then Nehemiah turns away for a moment and everything that could go wrong, does – which tells me that even the most spiritual saint is always in danger of falling on his face and he must be on constant guard, vigilant to maintain his relationship with God each day.

The enemy never sleeps. If you want to know what you have to do to fall, the answer is quite simple: do nothing. Live on yesterday's blessings and last year's word from the Lord. But to do well, to grow and move forward in Him, will require daily commitment of your time, energy, and devotion to Him and His ways.

I learn from Nehemiah and the leadership he established that ministering to people will always come with some built-in setbacks. Nehemiah had done everything right. The people had responded in kind. He'd left in charge those who were solid and proven in their faith. But people fail and the enemy is always there to escort them on their way down. If you're prone to discouragement, ministry is a tough place to be because the work in ministry is not done quickly. People don't learn something once and then know it for good. That would be great though, wouldn't it? We'd go through the Bible one time and say, "That's done. Now what do we do?" No, we stay at it because all of us are frail, in bodies of flesh, in a world of sin, and it is a battle to put on that new man. We need daily input, constant preaching, and continual reinforcement because the enemy wants to take us out.

So in Nehemiah's final chapter, he tells us about what he found: the struggles of the people, the difficulties he ran into, and how he had to be the enforcer. It must not be a good ministry to be the hammer and I don't think he wanted to be that. However, he wanted God to be pleased and was willing to make the difficult choices when he saw the wrongs around him. The first person to whom Nehemiah turns is this fellow Eliashib, the high priest. As the high priest, Eliashib was to set the tone for the spiritual practices and policies of the city. It was a place of great influence and leadership, but he failed. Instead of leading the people in the ways of the Lord, he became a follower of the world's influence.

Tobiah is the same person who, from the very beginning of this work of God, had stood in opposition. In 2:10, we read that he and a couple of his buddies were upset that someone was actually coming to Jerusalem to help the Jews, and were sure this was not going to work out for their benefit. Nine verses later, as the wall was beginning to be erected, it is he and some more of his friends who stood taunting the people. "You'll never build your way out of the rubbish," they cried. "You aren't talented enough. God can't use you. This is rebellion. Wait 'til the king hears about this."

By the time you come to chapter 4, the wall is half-built and Tobiah has organized an army of people to make bodily threats against the workers. "Stop building or die. You won't see us coming, but we're coming for you." In chapter 6, when the wall is finished, it is Tobiah who calls Nehemiah and says, "Look, I'm going to write to the king and say you're a seditionist, that you're trying to take over and build a kingdom for yourself. We have a lot of witnesses." And when that didn't work, he wrote him another letter saying, "Hey, let's have lunch and a summit meeting. We'll make peace." Nehemiah saw through all of the constant badgering by this enemy of God's people.

Nehemiah had never so much as let this man into the city. Back in chapter 2, he had set guards to watch out for the likes of him. When Nehemiah left town, Eliashib, the spiritual leader of the people, invites this Tobiah into the very temple itself. Here's the problem: If you have a spiritual leader who ignores the wisdom of God and begins to insert his friends into the life of the people, without any kind of standards or discernment, everyone suffers. Eliashib was that kind of guy. He could have been leading the people in the ways of the Lord, instead he embraces the very enemy of God's people and His work.

You cannot have overseers in ministry who are less interested in the spiritual well-being of those under them and more interested in what they can get from those people. "Oh, I know he's not doing very well with the Lord, but he sings really well. I know he's not in church regularly, but he's a great carpenter. I understand that he and his wife are having trouble, but you should hear him speak." Whenever we overlook sin to gain what we think is going to benefit us, everyone loses. That was Eliashib's problem. He compromised for the sake of his own benefit and he moved this enemy of God into the very temple storage chambers.

In the Old Testament, the temple was the only meeting place between God and man. You couldn't choose to meet with God wherever you wanted, you had to come seek Him at the tabernacle and, later, the temple. It was there that the offerings were made and only there that sinful man could approach a holy God. To keep the temple functioning, priests and worship leaders were paid in grain and fruit from the fields. These offerings of the people were kept in storage chambers. But under Eliashib's leadership, these chambers had become so empty that he could rent them out to others for his own gain. Tobiah, an outspoken opponent of God's work, now occupied the place that was once devoted to the things of God.

Whenever you set the Lord aside, the enemy has plenty of room to move in, doesn't he? There had been this great working of God, but now the fellows in charge are corrupt. As a result, the precious things of God are crowded out of the lives of the people by the deceptiveness of the world. The fruit of God's presence is no longer evident, and the place God once dwelled is an empty shell where the enemy dwells. What a picture.

Revival only comes when God's Word and His ways are preeminent. There are always a hundred ways for the enemy to move in once God's ways are set aside. The constant threat to our daily spiritual life is the desire of Satan to move Tobiah in. Friendship with the world provides that entry. In fact, the very sins that had taken the people down before, were taking them down again. Back in 9:2, the people had vowed that they were not going to repeat the sins of their fathers. "We don't want to do it like they did. We want to make a new deal with God." They wrote it out and signed it by the thousands. So what happened between then and now? One insight is given to us here in verse 3 where it appears much of the influence over the people came from those who were not truly devoted to the Lord, the "mixed multitude," as they were called. They were men like Tobiah who married into the faith but had no faith themselves. They may have had some kind of superficial relationship with God's people, but they had no relationship with God.

You find the mixed multitudes in Exodus leaving with the children of Israel. They weren't Jews, nor were they converts to the God of the Jews, but they saw that there was blessing with them and goodness to be had so they tagged along. As you read through Exodus, you see that often when dissent or rebellion was found, it was fomented by this group. Since they didn't know the Lord or His love, whenever things did not go their way, they were the first to complain and the first threatening to go back to Egypt where the "real life" was.

Every church has a mixed multitude in it. I've never yet been in a church that didn't. Not sold out to the Lord, they attend when necessary while always ready to point out the flaws, failures, and concerns they encounter. Like the mixed multitudes in the Scriptures, their counterparts in churches today are usually very charismatic and influential; people listen to them. Fortunately here Nehemiah arrives to declare, "We don't cater to these kind of folks. We cater to those who are hungry for the things of the Lord." When the mixed multitude leaves a church, that's not loss, that's blessed subtraction. And you'll find the same thing to be true with Tobiah. When Tobiah is removed from the temple, it's a good day in the life of the people and things are about to get much better!

> *Then after certain days I obtained leave from the king, and I came to Jerusalem and discovered the evil that Eliashib had done for Tobiah, in preparing a room for him in the courts of the house of God. And it grieved me bitterly; therefore I threw all the household goods of Tobiah out of the room.*
>
> *–Nehemiah 13:6b-8*

Whatever brought Nehemiah back – and I suspect it was his great love for the people – he soon got wind of what was going on and, as a true spiritual leader who cared for the flock, the news broke his heart. He couldn't fathom how someone could get in and do this to the people in such a short period of time.

Notice Nehemiah's response was to quickly restore order. His anger was not in self-defense. His anger was righteous. He saw the Lord's name being offended and God's people being abused, and he wasn't going to put up with this for five more minutes. Paul had a man in ministry with him named Demas. He traveled with Paul to the Colossian area, working and serving with him. When Paul wrote the Philemon letter, in verse 24 of that little book, he called Demas a "fellow laborer," someone he loved ministering with. Yet by the time Paul is on death row, awaiting his execution, he writes in his last letter to Timothy, "Demas has forsaken me, having loved this present world, and has departed for Thessalonica—Crescens for Galatia, Titus for Dalmatia" (2 Timothy 4:10).

Paul would continue, but Demas would not. Nehemiah would continue, but Tobiah and Eliashib would not. Nehemiah's the real deal. He makes tough decisions to care for God's flock and the first thing he does is start spring cleaning at the temple. Tobiah comes home from work and all of his furniture is sitting at the curb. "Hey, I paid to the end of the month."

"Tough, buddy. You're no longer living here."

"Who said?"

"Nehemiah did."

Nehemiah may not be politically correct, but you sure like his diligence, don't you? This guy is a true dedicated and loyal servant of God.

> *Then I commanded them to cleanse the rooms; and I brought back into them the articles of the house of God, with the grain offering and the frankincense.*
>
> *–Nehemiah 13:9*

After fumigating the place, Nehemiah returned the storerooms to the use God had given them. He puts first things first, the eternal things first, at all cost. Learn well the fact that the alliances you make determine your character. Nehemiah was only good at making friends with those who sought the Lord. To the rest he brought the Word of God.

Paul warned the Ephesians, "And have no fellowship with the unfruitful works of darkness, but rather expose them" (Ephesians 5:11). He wrote to the Romans, "Now I urge you, brethren, note those who cause divisions and offenses, contrary to the doctrine which you learned, and avoid them" (Romans 16:17). He told the Corinthians, "I wrote to you in my epistle not to keep company with sexually immoral people. Yet I certainly did not mean with the sexually immoral people of this world, or with the covetous, or extortioners, or idolaters, since then you would need to go out of the world. But now I have written to you not to keep company with anyone named a brother, who is sexually immoral, or covetous, or an idolater, or a reviler, or a drunkard, or an extortioner—not even to eat with such a person" (1 Corinthians 5:9-11). In 2 Thessalonians 3:6, he told the saints, "But we command you, brethren, in the name of our Lord Jesus Christ, that you withdraw from every brother who walks disorderly and not according to the tradition which he received from us." Then added in 2 Thessalonians 3:14-15, "And if anyone does not obey our word in this epistle, note that person, and do not keep company with him, that he may be ashamed. Yet do not count him as an enemy, but admonish him as a brother." Nehemiah knew this was not a time to make nice, it was time for God's people to be separate from the world.

Eliashib was supposedly the spiritual leader of the people, but he was making deals with the devil in the back room. He's emptying out the holy rooms of God and filling them with unholy people, one room at a time. Nehemiah was courageous enough to declare, "That's not going to happen here."

> *I also realized that the portions for the Levites had not been given them; for each of the Levites and the singers who did the work had gone back to his field. So I contended with the rulers, and said, "Why is the house of God forsaken?" And I gathered them together and set them in their place. Then all Judah brought the tithe of the grain and the new wine and the oil to the storehouse. And I appointed as treasurers over the storehouse Shelemiah the priest and Zadok the scribe, and of the Levites, Pedaiah; and next to them was Hanan the son of Zaccur, the son of Mattaniah; for they were considered faithful, and their task was to distribute to their brethren.*
>
> *–Nehemiah 13:10-13*

Nehemiah's second concern was support for the priests

and the singers in the work of the Lord had been set aside by the corrupt leadership of men like Eliashib. There was no longer faithfulness, no longer commitment, and no longer a love for the things of God. The people viewed Eliashib and men like him as crooks that they could not trust, and so they left.

Never place in authority in the church someone who has brilliant qualifications in every area except their spiritual life. Churches sometimes mistakenly do that. They'll hire the best accountant, the best lawyer, or the best administrator, but they don't care too much about their spiritual lives. I'd rather have one serving with me who simply loved Jesus and sought only to bless Him.

In 1 Samuel 2, you can read of Eli who was also a high priest. When the people came to bring their offerings to the Lord, Eli's sons would bring large hooks and rip out the best portion of the meat for themselves. The result was that the people hated coming, because rather than meeting a loving Lord, they met crooked men who were supposed to represent Him, but didn't. They didn't hate God; they just hated His representatives. Eli eventually lost his ministry because God said that he hadn't sought to restrain his sons and their wicked influence over God's people.

In Jesus' day, it was the temple Pharisees who committed the same atrocious sins with the same expected result. They would refuse your offering, saying they found a flaw or fault with it, and they would demand you exchanged your hard-earned money for special temple coins that they would give you for a fee.

In 12:44, Nehemiah wrote that Judah rejoiced over the priests and the Levites who were ministering to them and they brought the firstfruits into the storehouse because they wanted a place where they could meet with God. One chapter later and that has all stopped. But Nehemiah quickly sets about putting things back in order. In verse 11, we read he "contended with the rulers" for the way the money was gathered and spent. The word "contended" means "to scream back and forth." In other words, Nehemiah took these guys to task. "Hey, what do you guys think you're doing? Why is the place shut down? Where are all the priests? Who's responsible for this?" Welcome home, Nehemiah!

In so doing, he returned all of the priests and servants to their positions telling them they were to stay at their positions serving the Lord. Verse 12 tells us that when Judah saw the corruption was gone, the people indeed returned; returned to giving, returned to worship, and were blessed once again.

We'll soon read some other descriptions of Nehemiah's action. "I cursed them. I struck them. I pulled out their hair. And I made them swear by God." No wonder we like Nehemiah so much. He runs a tight ship. Cross the line with him and you are going to hear about it.

> *Remember me, O my God, concerning this, and do not wipe out my good deeds that I have done for the house of my God, and for its services!*
>
> *–Nehemiah 13:14*

This was a tough assignment, a tough road for Nehemiah to walk. He was swimming upstream. He was alone with no committee on his side, but was interested in blessing the Lord. This prayer will be repeated in verses 22 and 30 because Nehemiah knows that the only approval he's going to find at this point is from God. This wasn't a prayer for personal reward. He was just asking God to bless the radical changes, to have them take effect, and to be sure the people would be blessed. We need this kind of leadership in the church today. We don't need guys compromising their faith so they can be politically correct. I just want to be correct with God. I just want one thumb up – His.

I think the danger is finding people less committed than we are and then feeling good about our spiritual standing compared to theirs. Then we can do whatever we want without much conviction because everyone we know is worse off than we are. But the standard isn't our buddies' behavior; the standard is God's Word. Nehemiah was the only guy willing to stick with what God had said.

There can't be relative holiness in our lives. You can't talk about holiness and not pursue it. You can't preach about it without living it. If it isn't part of your life, you're fooling yourself. The warning of this final chapter is the necessity of daily diligence. You should be going forward not backward, but it is much easier to go backwards.

> *In those days I saw people in Judah treading wine presses on the Sabbath, and bringing in sheaves, and loading donkeys with wine, grapes, figs, and all kinds of burdens, which they brought into Jerusalem on the Sabbath day. And I warned them about the day on which they were selling provisions.*
>
> *–Nehemiah 13:15*

The Sabbath was a covenant God had made with His people, Israel, back in Exodus. Its purpose was basically this: One day a week they were to set aside their commerce, business, gain, and worldly ambition to stop and realize God was the One who provided for all of their needs. It was to be a day dedicated to rest, fellowship, and the things of the Lord, a reminder that they didn't need to kill themselves to provide for themselves. They were to work hard on other days, but, in the end, God was the One who provided all things.

When Nehemiah left and the temple closed, the giving stopped, the teaching dried up, and the holiness of the Sabbath was hardly of concern to anyone. What they became interested in was what everyone in the world was interested in – gain. "Let's get while we can." The Sabbath had become just another workday.

> *Men of Tyre dwelt there also, who brought in fish and all kinds of goods, and sold them on the Sabbath to the*

> *children of Judah, and in Jerusalem.*
>
> *–Nehemiah 13:16*

Tyre was hundreds of miles up the coast. Nehemiah couldn't have been angrier. Look how he piles up the words: "on the Sabbath," "to the children of Judah," and "in Jerusalem."

> *Then I contended with the nobles of Judah, and said to them, "What evil thing is this that you do, by which you profane the Sabbath day?"*
>
> *–Nehemiah 13:17*

Notice that Nehemiah doesn't confront the men of Tyre. He goes after the rulers of Judah. It's always the leadership that sets the tone and the men of Tyre were leading these leaders. When the world begins to set your tone and your priorities, when you care more about the things of the world than the things of the Lord, God's people will falter.

Nehemiah comes yelling and screaming. He lets them have it. He steps up and speaks out to declare, "This is wrong!" He loves the people enough to say something. Often we are more interested in being well-liked than serving the Lord. So we see things but say nothing. Nehemiah saw and spoke up!

> *"Did not your fathers do thus, and did not our God bring all this disaster on us and on this city? Yet you bring added wrath on Israel by profaning the Sabbath."*
>
> *–Nehemiah 13:18*

Nehemiah reminded the people this was exactly the kind of thing that had brought God's judgment upon their ancestors. Now they were beginning to store up judgment again. "Don't you get it?" he says. "When are you going to wake up? Who's in charge here?"

> *So it was, at the gates of Jerusalem, as it began to be dark before the Sabbath, that I commanded the gates to be shut, and charged that they must not be opened till after the Sabbath. Then I posted some of my servants at the gates, so that no burdens would be brought in on the Sabbath day.*
>
> *–Nehemiah 13:19*

Nehemiah's solution was very interesting because it was political in the sense that he was the governor. He had absolute authority. Did he change a ruler's heart by doing this? Probably not. There's no way to forcibly make someone righteous. On the other hand, those in leadership certainly have the obligation to set the tone and the practices for the people who follow. Whether the people liked it or not didn't really matter. God would like it.

From a governmental standpoint, Nehemiah took the lead. He contended with the rulers. He kept commerce out. "We will honor the Sabbath," he declared. "There will be no buying and selling, and I'll put my own soldiers at the gates to make sure of it."

Nehemiah couldn't force righteousness. Yet leadership has the capacity to make policies and practices that, when implemented, will bring honor to the Lord. What it does to the heart is God's issue, but what form it takes outwardly was Nehemiah's responsibility.

> *Now the merchants and sellers of all kinds of wares lodged outside Jerusalem once or twice. Then I warned them, and said to them, "Why do you spend the night around the wall? If you do so again, I will lay hands on you!" From that time on they came no more on the Sabbath.*
>
> *–Nehemiah 13:20-21*

A couple of weeks passed and the merchants were still

clamoring to get into town to sell on the Sabbath. Nehemiah promised to "lay his hands" on them – and I don't think he meant to pray for them! I love his passion. He is committed to doing things right for the sake of the people. This isn't winning him any points. This isn't gaining him any money. This isn't promoting him in the culture. This is putting him on his knees, saying, "Oh, God, remember these things and use them." But he's interested in the people to the point where he will do what it takes to accomplish God's best and he wants to do it for their benefit.

Having dealt with the leaders of Judah in verse 17, Nehemiah next deals directly with the merchants. With his dealing with them being so blunt, you might look at Nehemiah and think, "The guy needs anger management classes," or, "I thought you were a believer." But Nehemiah loved the Lord and his anger was totally righteous.

> *And I commanded the Levites that they should cleanse themselves, and that they should go and guard the gates, to sanctify the Sabbath day. Remember me, O my God, concerning this also, and spare me according to the greatness of Your mercy!*
>
> *–Nehemiah 13:22*

This is an interesting prayer because one of two things is going on. Either, as he asks God to spare him by His great mercy, Nehemiah was encountering the wrath of all of the businessmen who had lost money because of his policies – or, because the word mercy speaks of not getting what one deserves, it is possible that Nehemiah felt responsible for the backsliding of the nation. Maybe he felt he hadn't done enough to leave it in a better spiritual state. Either one of those things can be true from the context.

In any event, Nehemiah was only interested in the Lord being honored. It wasn't popularity. It wasn't pride. It wasn't self-interest. If you're after popularity, pride, or self-interest, you will probably not confront someone living in sin. You will instead send them to church and let someone else deal with it or simply ignore it all together. But if you're interested in pleasing the Lord, sometimes the best you can do for someone is to tell them that they're way out of line and that it's not going to fly with you. It's a faithfulness that we need in the church. I'm not talking about sin-sniffers or being anointed for the "ministry of rebuke," but there are people who live in sin and they should hear that from you. You shouldn't look the other way. You shouldn't sweep it under the rug. They shouldn't be over at your house having dinner. You should be telling them to get right with God.

> *In those days I also saw Jews who had married women of Ashdod, Ammon, and Moab. And half of their children spoke the language of Ashdod, and could not speak the language of Judah, but spoke according to the language of one or the other people.*
>
> *–Nehemiah 13:23-24*

The inter-marrying of the Jews with the nations surrounding them is an often seen practice throughout the Bible, a practice God forbids. It is not that God is prejudiced. His only concern is the spiritual well-being of His people. He wanted to keep them for Himself. He taught them to be in fellowship with one another, to marry those who loved God as they did, to not place themselves in a position where other things could compromise their relationship with Him.

Due to intermarriage, the kids in Jerusalem weren't reading Hebrew. They couldn't read the Bible. They were learning the lessons and the ways of the world. Back when the people were repenting in chapter 10, their hearts were different: "We're not getting involved with the world around us anymore. We're not giving them our kids to marry. We're not taking kids from them to marry into our families. We're going to commit ourselves to the things of God." Now, though, with the daily diligence gone, things had changed: "No, he's not saved, but look how good-looking he is! No, she's not saved, but she's not against God." And into the world we go. We compromise and we lose that edge; it dulls the relationship that God wants us to have with Him.

> *So I contended with them and cursed them, struck some of them and pulled out their hair, and made them swear by God, saying, "You shall not give your daughters as wives to their sons, nor take their daughters for your sons or yourselves."*
>
> *–Nehemiah 13:25*

"So I contended..." There's that screaming word again. "Don't marry the heathen!" Nehemiah said. "Swear before God!" Don't you wish you could solve everything like this? We're so tactful, aren't we? We should be tactful, but we should also be holy.

In 2 Samuel 12, Nathan was a young prophet whom the Lord sent to confront David about his sin with Bathsheba. I'm thinking that is not an assignment Nathan was looking forward to. David, the all powerful, could kill him on the spot. Nathan most likely would have preferred to say nothing, but he was obedient to the Lord and God used him to bring David to repentance.

Near the beginning of His public ministry in John 2 and again nearing the end of it in Matthew 21, Jesus walked into the temple in Jerusalem and turned over the tables of those selling their wares. He chased them with whips. He screamed at them, "'My house shall be called a house of prayer,' but you have made it a 'den of thieves'" (Matthew 21:13). That's not Jesus meek and mild. That's not baby Jesus. That's Jesus angry that man had so corrupted the things of God and, in so doing, was turning away the hearts of many from His love. He made His point well known with the vendors.

We certainly never set out to purposefully hurt feelings, yet Jesus made clear that drastic spiritual needs require drastic actions. He said "If your right eye causes you to sin, pluck it out and cast it from you; for it is more profitable for you that one of your members perish, than for your whole body to be cast into hell" (Matthew 5:29). There are things that are so valuable and of such great importance that you should do whatever it takes to be sure that you attain it in the end. Your eternity is that important! So Jesus encouraged His disciples to, "Get rid of whatever keeps you from God." That's the kind of drama Nehemiah finds himself in. The contending, the striking, and the pulling of the hair were cultural, but he used those expressions to get his point across. What is at stake for you and for us as God's nation is being threatened by our sinful choices. Drastic measures are needed to get us back on track so we don't make the same foolish mistakes of our past.

> *"Did not Solomon king of Israel sin by these things? Yet among many nations there was no king like him, who was beloved of his God; and God made him king over all Israel. Nevertheless pagan women caused even him to sin. Should we then hear of your doing all this great evil, transgressing against our God by marrying pagan women?"*
>
> *–Nehemiah 13:26-27*

Nehemiah's point is that even men like Solomon – wiser than any man who ever lived, along with being powerful, rich, successful, and in fellowship with God for years – fell. Solomon, in later years, was found worshiping other gods, far removed from the God he once knew. Yet from the book of Ecclesiastes, especially the final few chapters, we believe Solomon returned to the God of his youth after many wasted years. "It doesn't matter how strong you might have been or how wise you think you are," Nehemiah says. "The wisest guy in the world, the most blessed man around, couldn't stand when he let this area of his life begin to fall."

And one of the sons of Joiada, the son of Eliashib the high priest, was a son-in-law of Sanballat the Horonite; therefore I drove him from me.

–Nehemiah 13:28

The son of the high priest had also compromised himself, marrying into Sanballat's family. Sanballat was the other enemy of God and His people who, along with Tobiah, had opposed this work and caused much grief from the beginning. He was next in the crosshairs of Nehemiah's wrath and he too is moved out of the temple and away from God's people.

Nehemiah has certainly been busy since he returned! He's been confronting, contending, cursing, hair-pulling, threatening, striking, and running people out of town. But I love his passion; he's a man sold out for the Lord and will do whatever he can to make sure God's people walk with God. We don't need relative holiness. We need the pursuit of God's holiness. We're weak and we're not always going to do well. I understand that. God, help us not to sweep sin under the rug, but rather confront it and seek to be delivered from it.

Remember them, O my God, because they have defiled the priesthood and the covenant of the priesthood and the Levites. Thus I cleansed them of everything pagan. I also assigned duties to the priests and the Levites, each to his service, and to bringing the wood offering and the firstfruits at appointed times. Remember me, O my God, for good!

–Nehemiah 13:29-31

Nehemiah finally restores the priests back to their service in the temple. He gives direction and wisdom and brings organization to all. Through the drastic steps of one man, a nation was spared the further judgment of God and was instead brought into a place of great blessing.

As a pastor, I learn from chapter 13 that ministry work

is never finished. There are constant needs to be encouraged to stay the course, to keep your eyes on Jesus, believe His Word, and obey Him. To those of you who seek to be in leadership, let me say this to you: be sure you are leading the flock. Don't let the flock lead you. Rather set the standard, walk with God, and let Him and His ways be what is most important to you. If you fail because of that course, then go ahead and fail, because in heaven, you'll be glad you did. You are called to please the Lord. You've got to stand with Him, and for Him, and that requires a full commitment.

Paul warned the Corinthians, "Therefore let him who thinks he stands take heed lest he fall" (1 Corinthians 10:12). We must be careful to maintain lifestyles and practices that draw us closer to Him. Just reading Jesus' letters to the churches in Revelation 2-3 should convince you of the need we have to daily seek after Him.

Sometimes it takes radical steps to get back on track. You have to chase Tobiah off. Nehemiah was faithful to the end. "Remember me, O my God, for good," he prayed. And God answered his prayer because 2,500 years later, you have just finished his book, which he was led to write by the leading of the Holy Spirit, to help us learn the lessons of service, faith, and obedience. Now walk like Nehemiah and let's see what God will do with you!